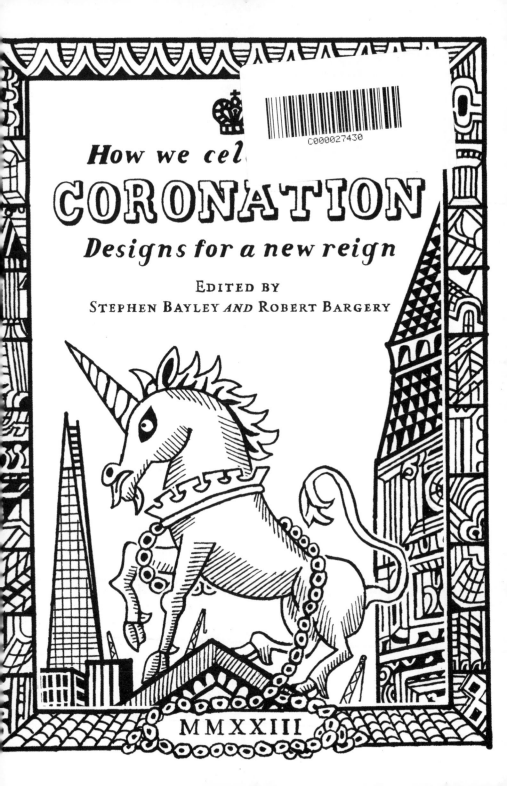

How we cel...

CORONATION

Designs for a new reign

EDITED BY
STEPHEN BAYLEY *AND* ROBERT BARGERY

MMXXIII

CONTENTS

Introduction   4

INTRODUCTION

To mark the Coronation of George VI in May 1937, Robert Byron wrote a blistering piece in *The Architectural Review* criticising the razing of historic buildings in London. Entitled *How We Celebrate the Coronation*, it was later published as a booklet and helped to shift opinion in favour of building conservation. Nearly a century on, it still makes scintillating reading.

As we enter a new reign, a novel experience for almost all of us and a natural time both to take stock and to think ahead, we have borrowed Byron's title for this charitable publication to mark the Coronation of His Majesty the King in May 2023. We invited around fifty distinguished people to contribute pieces on aspects of the built environment in the United Kingdom that they thought could be improved. We promised free rein, and no sensitivity reader.

The net effect, we hope, will be to provoke debate and to spark action. And, more generally, to open eyes. There is still a need for this. In 1963, Hubert de Cronin Hastings, editor of *The Architectural Review*, wrote that we (by which he meant the English) were blind to the physical consequences of squalor. 'Blind to wire, dustbins, milk bottles, broken railings, bungaloidia, charapox, Banker's Georgian, Pseudish, Concrete-arterial, by-pass industrial. Blind to the good as well as the bad. Blind to our own heritage. Blind, even while we crawl all over them, to the lessons in urbanity furnished by our neighbours, starting with the Italians.'

The Royal Fine Art Commission Trust has long sought to remedy this by promoting visual awareness. From our Learning to See initiative for schoolchildren in the 1990s to our Building Beauty Awards, presented for the first time in 2022, our aim is to encourage critical appreciation of our built environment as a prelude to demanding better.

Some things, of course, are now better, far better. Anyone who remembers the courtyard of Somerset House – one of Europe's great civic spaces – as a car park for the taxman, or Horse Guards Parade as a car park for civil servants, will know that to be true. And it may be said that we plan our countryside, if not our cities, rather better than the Italians. But equally, we know that everywhere we go we are assailed by signage and its infantilising inanities; that once-elegant telephone boxes are now no more than gaudy advertising hoardings; that the area outside the National Gallery is now a kind of anarchic strip abandoned to amplified buskers and other incivilities; that even the very setting of His Majesty's Coronation is hideously marred by the security junk that clutters the area between the Palace of Westminster and Westminster Abbey.

Some of that will be spruced up and made good for the Coronation. We are at any rate better than we used to be at Potemkin cosmetics: the King will avoid the indignities suffered by George IV, who on returning to Carlton House from Westminster Hall after his Coronation in 1821 found his path blocked by two overturned carriages, was forced into a detour down brothel-ridden backstreets and ended up having to cross a foetid culvert by a wooden bridge so rickety that it was out of bounds even to wheelbarrows.

We manage better than that, but we can manage better still. These pages are intended as a kind of *vade mecum*, to help show us how. Some of its ideas, we hope, will please the King, capture the imagination of his people and prod his ministers into action. As an immediate measure, we commend Ed Vaizey's suggestion that the late Royal Fine Art Commission, that expert independent adjudicator on matters of visual amenity, be re-established. It was created in 1924, the first act of Britain's first Labour Government. What better way to celebrate its centenary, and to demonstrate commitment to the quality of the world around us, than to bring it back to life?

Stephen Bayley
CHAIRMAN
Royal Fine Art Commission Trust

Robert Bargery
EXECUTIVE DIRECTOR
Royal Fine Art Commission Trust

URBAN HOUSEKEEPING

Lord Foster of Thames Bank O.M.

(b. 1935. ROBERT WATSON-WATT DEMONSTRATES RADAR)

Architect nonpareil. President of The Royal Fine Art Commission Trust.

MY MOST RECENT TRAVELS HAVE TAKEN ME to Bilbao, London, Paris, Madrid and New York. All have impressive civic spaces: intimate streets, wide boulevards and humanly-scaled squares. Think of these as urban rooms in which the sky is the ceiling. They define the DNA of the place, differing according to its particular scale and character. The second common characteristic is sadly negative. All are blighted by a relatively recent attack of urban paraphernalia, temporary in its intent but near permanent in its reality: a motley collection of steel barriers, plastic cones and signs, garbage bags and wheelie bins.

This proliferation throughout the urbanised world is a visual plague. It seems as if entire populaces have become so accustomed to it that they take the collective ugliness for granted. I accept that some of these interventions are necessary and that they need to command attention by using strident colours. Most could be more discreetly toned, but these too often use colours that scream for attention. There is also the question of design and materials. Perhaps in the past most of these eruptions would come and go swiftly. Now they seem to linger long beyond their need, with pavements acting as a kind of parking lot for their storage. I have instanced a small number of cities, but it is a global problem and goes beyond city centres. On my travels I have snapped examples. My latest one, which I saw standing in line for a ski-lift in an Alpine resort, is of bright yellow plastic barriers. Sometimes I suspect that they are a permanent substitute for a post-occupancy design correction.

As a student in the nineteen-fifties, I was impressed by the *Outrage* campaign of *The Architectural Review*, and I avidly followed a small band of writer-illustrators who railed against the civic vandalism that was threatening urban landscapes across the nation. Perhaps it is now time for the media to raise the level of public awareness through a campaign for Urban Housekeeping. We would never tolerate lingering piles of plastic-wrapped garbage in our domestic spaces. Why should we do so in the public outdoor rooms of our cities?

SAVE VICTORIA TOWER GARDENS

Hal Moggridge C.B.E.

(b. 1936. KEYNES' *GENERAL THEORY OF EMPLOYMENT, INTEREST AND MONEY* PUBLISHED)

Co-founder of Colvin & Moggridge landscape architects.

POLITICIANS SHOULD STOP GRABBING urban parkland for their favoured building projects. A glaring instance is Victoria Tower Gardens beside the Palace of Westminster, which Parliament is considering stealing from the public.

In 2016 the then Prime Minister, David Cameron, briefed by two now-retired politicians careless of people or place, decided without analysis to seize the park for a Holocaust memorial and underground museum, overriding Westminster City Council's refusal of consent, ignoring the then Foreign Secretary's assertion that 'we are a rules-based country and we stick to those rules' and contravening the 1900 London County Council Act which requires the land to be kept 'as a public garden', a provision upheld recently by the High Court.

National planning policy requires that 'existing open space...should not be built on unless...replaced by equivalent or better provision'. But no alternative parkland is proposed. The Gardens would be monitored by uniformed 'security operatives', discouraging informal recreational use by local residents, many of them low-income families without other outdoor space. The wildlife of the splendid plane trees would be disturbed, a quiet resting place for tired tourists smothered. Crowded assembly before democratic demonstrations or for state events like Her late Majesty's lying-in-state would become impossible.

If needed, an evocative memorial in scale with the Gardens' other memorials could be added near the north-east corner, where a small riverside contemplation garden could also be created. But if this huge memorial were to be built, it would express nothing of the sorrows and horrors of the Holocaust. It would stand instead as a memorial to an intransigent parliamentary administration which had decided to set the horrible precedent of using parliamentary power to shove an inappropriate building into precious parkland seized from the urban population, so denying them innocent contact with nature. It would forever express political nastiness and the denigration of British democracy.

DESIGN LITERACY AND THINKING AHEAD

Sir Terry Farrell C.B.E.

(b. 1938. CHAMBERLAIN RETURNS FROM MEETING HITLER IN MUNICH WITH
AN ASSURANCE OF 'PEACE FOR OUR TIME')

*Architect and urban designer whose buildings include Asia's largest railway station
and London's finest essays in Postmodernism.*

PLACES WOULD BE GREATLY IMPROVED if the people who make
decisions about our built environment, such as planning committee members
and highway engineers, were design literate. Newly-elected councillors already
receive mandatory training on financial and legal duties; design training should
be added to that. After all, it is in all our interests that everyone who makes
decisions about the built environment is able to read plans at the very least.

Places will become great only if there is civic leadership, whether from
politicians, community groups or built environment professionals. It is
individuals who make the difference, not policies, and we need more leaders
who truly care about the built environment. Who is doing the visionary thinking
in this country? There have been good examples recently in places like Brent,
Croydon, Birmingham and Manchester. That is often down to strong leadership
and the right skills in local authorities, but local enterprise partnerships and
neighbourhood forums also play a part. We can learn from countries like
France, Sweden, Denmark and the US (particularly New York) where top-
level guidance is given on the shape and form of the built environment, often
with the help of private-sector professionals. This would place less pressure on
dwindling resources in planning departments, give more certainty from the
outset to developers and create better-quality places for us all.

At the moment we need more housing, but in a democratic society the only
way of persuading those already housed of the benefits of more housing is by
presenting a credible vision of the future, by thinking ahead rather than reacting
to events. Take the impact of flooding on new housing. Prevention through
adaptation is far more effective than control through mitigation. It is notable
that one outcome of recent flooding has been a clamour for 'more planning', in
a culture previously hostile to the very idea of planning. We are realising that
freedom and planning are not opposed, that planning can liberate us.

SKYLINE CLEANSING

Lord Rees of Ludlow O.M., F.R.S.

(b. 1942. USA EMBARKS ON THE MANHATTAN PROJECT, CULMINATING IN THE ATOMIC BOMB)

*Cosmologist and astrophysicist. Astronomer Royal since 1995
and President of the Royal Society from 2005 to 2010.*

UNTIL THE MID-TWENTIETH CENTURY, the most prominent buildings in London served public purposes, and gave all citizens a feeling of 'ownership'. Supreme among them were the cathedrals and churches; and Barry's Houses of Parliament. But there were also the great museums and railway stations.

But now the skyline is scarred by 'tower blocks'. Some may have architectural merit viewed as stand-alone edifices, but they are jumbled together in an uncoordinated fashion. More than that, they send a depressing signal about society's priorities. They aren't 'public' buildings. They are mainly banks and expensive apartments: displays of wealth and celebrations of finance.

The one consolation is that many of these monstrosities aren't built to last. Their lifespan might be fifty years. So perhaps, before the twenty-first century ends, the skyline will be 'cleansed', reverting to one dominated by buildings – new as well as old – that we can celebrate aesthetically and as democratic citizens.

DROP HOUSING TARGETS

Sir Stuart Lipton

(b. 1942. BATTLE OF EL ALAMEIN)

*Developer of over twenty million square feet of London property and first
Chairman of The Commission for Architecture and the Built Environment.*

DOES ANYONE CARE ABOUT INADEQUATE HOUSING? The socio-economic and direct financial cost it imposes is vast, through (for example) lost productivity from ill-health, a greater burden on public services and increased crime. Our fear of building enough good new homes affects not just those on low incomes but those on decent salaries, who have little disposable income left after using half of it to keep a roof over their heads. We have brilliant, inventive people in this country, and four of the top universities in the world; but those people need decent affordable housing if they are to stay.

We need 500,000 houses a year to make homes affordable, produce a functioning free market and remedy obsolescence. One answer is higher densities and greater use of brownfield sites, allied to much stricter controls on greenbelt use. Another is to stop imposing housing targets on local authorities and instead offer them inducements, such as giving them a share of the five taxes imposed on development for them to use for the benefit of local communities. In London, half of section 106 tax revenue is unused. No-one has put an exact figure on that, but informed commentators suggest it is close to £1bn.

With skilled town planning, we can create places that bring pride, aspiration and a sense of belonging. By returning to the traditions of city and town squares and village greens, and by investing in quality architecture, we can recover a sense of purpose and motivation in our lives.

MAKE BUILDINGS WORK TOGETHER

Sir Simon Jenkins

(b. 1943. UTILITY FURNITURE INTRODUCED TO BRITISH MARKET)

Former editor of The Times and Chairman of The National Trust. One of the outstanding journalists of his era and one of heritage's most articulate voices.

BRITAIN HAS MADE VAST STRIDES IN PUBLIC CONCERN for its architecture since the 1930s. Planning is no longer just let rip. Successive acts of parliament have gradually accepted that the past of the built environment is integral to the present. But just as architecture has merited legal protection, so the threat to it has grown ever more challenging in one way: Britain has failed completely to regulate the setting of buildings, their relationship with the spaces round them, the environment and landscape.

Most stark is the inability to order the siting of very large buildings. Towers sprout at random across almost every British city as is simply not so across most of the continent. Subtleties of clustering, proportion and balance are ignored, largely because of property interests. The London skyline is the most pockmarked of any city in Europe. Scarcely a vista is free of jarring intrusion.

The same applies to the custodianship of urban streets, residential or commercial. New buildings ignore the size and presentation of their neighbours. Streets once lined with individual properties of character are now sweeps of concrete and glass. Where shops and cafeterias caused people to stop, look and talk, blank walls now force them to scurry by. The busiest streets in London now almost all date from a century or more ago, such as Brick Lane, Portobello Road, Camden High Street and Borough Market. Architects have lost the art of creating amenable public spaces.

We should not only blame architects, who in the eternal phrase are 'only obeying orders'. The fault lies with the planners and local and national politicians who ignore the appeal of old buildings and the toxic effect of towers and slabs on the spaces round them. Correcting this requires an alert and informed public with the right to be consulted on buildings that will surround them all their lives. Britons should learn about architecture, how it works and how it affects their use of the city. If people will not talk, then money will, and bad buildings will result.

HUMANISTIC SPACE

Cecil Balmond O.B.E.

(b. 1943. CHURCHILL, ROOSEVELT AND STALIN CONVENE IN TEHRAN
TO PLAN OPERATION OVERLORD)

Renaissance man who straddles the disciplines of art, design and engineering. With Sir Anish Kapoor, he designed the Orbit at the Queen Elizabeth Olympic Park.

A CITY MUST BE A CATALYST for an imagined better future. The mute fabric we see everywhere should be animated with a sense of 'place'. To do this, let's expand laterally in our dense centres, getting rid of the pavement strip conceptually and opening up the ground floor of buildings lining the street to create passageways or broad corridors for wider access. Instead of coercing us into linear travel, the street should branch here and there into the dense fabric, creating transparency at ground level, coloured movement thresholds, vistas, spaces for art and internal landscape and room for amenities such as drinking fountains, bathroom facilities and small recycling units. Buildings would have a limited entry point on the ground floor; the first floor would house main access and security and be a jump zone for environmental data gathering. Urban buildings are already becoming multi-functional, mixed social hubs. As residential use increases, an activated ground zone will be a social necessity.

The lateral idea of breaking down narrow confines should spread to the rivers that run through the heart of many cities. Over time, development has turned its back on the water. Let's break through embankment walls and launch viewing platforms over the water's edge, linking people with the water that sustains them.

SHARING THE NATION'S WEALTH

Jules Lubbock

(b. 1943. WARSAW GHETTO UPRISING)

Professor Emeritus in the History of Art at the University of Essex, Lubbock is an impossible-to-categorise twenty-first century man-of-letters.

COMMODITY, FIRMNESS AND DELIGHT, the Vitruvian triad, fails to mention the two most important Elements of Architecture - Money and Power. Only the richest individuals, institutions and the state have the cash to lavish upon fine craftsmanship and to build on a grand scale in the best places. This fact has put its stamp upon the United Kingdom and upon London its capital. His Majesty inherits a dozen architectural masterpieces – houses, palaces, castles, not to mention landscapes and gardens, and has several more at his disposal. The entire *quartier* of British government and state ceremonial from the Palace of Westminster with its Palatine Chapel and Westminster Abbey, imitating Solomon's Temple and Palace, to Buckingham Palace in the west incorporating the Mall, Green Park, Hyde Park, the Palace of Whitehall, St. James's Park and Palace, belonged to the mediaeval royal domain and covers over 1,000 acres, double the square mileage of Hampstead Heath.

This raises the question of what Thomas Aquinas, following Plato and Aristotle, called distributive justice: how should the 'wealth of nations' be equitably shared? Plato believed that the richest should possess no more than five times the wealth of the poorest. Aristotle agreed but preferred not to put too precise a figure on it; nonetheless he argued that if inequality were too great the unity of society would be fragmented and national security jeopardised. Plato's idea implies a top personal income of £100,000 and no homes larger than 3,000 sq.ft. More than enough, surely, for a very good life?

Apart from the ethical benefits of greater equality, how would my modest proposal affect our architecture and environment, subjects dear to King Charles's heart? All private country houses, the royal estate included, would join the National Trust and English Heritage. His Majesty has already played his part in rescuing Dumfries House and its magnificent Chippendale furnishings for the nation. His neo-vernacular developments in Truro, Newquay and Poundbury are models for the design of houses for all, living side-by-side in a distributionally just society.

The Enlightenment philosopher David Hume argued that a 'civilised monarchy' is the most favourable for the arts to flourish. King Charles is the most civilised monarch we have ever had: our modern Solomon, our philosopher king.

FREEDOM TO DRIVE

Nick Mason C.B.E.

(b. 1944. V-1 "DOODLEBUGS" DROPPED ON LONDON)

As drummer of Pink Floyd, Mason, who trained as an architect, has sold 250 million records.

OH FOR THOSE HALCYON DAYS when the motorcar had recently taken over from the horse; when the Bentley Boys drove into Berkeley Square and jumped out of their cars for an evening of drinking and jolly banter, before returning to their motor vehicles to race the Blue Train down to the French Riviera. They'd be lucky to make Croydon today.

The innocence! No concept of breathalysers, parking tickets, congestion charges or car clamps. Perhaps most important of all, streets could accommodate the width of their cars. A distant memory. Only the streets remain the same: as wide as they were but now with a plethora of speed bumps, yellow lines and a giddying festoon of instructions on parking and speed restrictions. Driving needs to be better than sitting in a soup of stationary vehicles and sometimes conflicting instructions, or continually trying to squeeze past that Ocado delivery van.

Something can be done. Some years ago, Volkswagen presented their version of a supercar. Designated the XL1, it was in effect a micro-supercar. This machine not only looked fabulous but could travel 100 kilometres on one litre of fuel. With the addition of green fuel it would be a far better option than overweight monsters with giant eco-unfriendly batteries and over-optimistic mileage ranges. With a good navigation system, virtually any journey would be much quicker and a lot more relaxing. Add driverless technology and almost all that street furniture could be tossed to one side.

FIFTEEN MINUTES TO SAVE THE CITY

Peter Murray C.B.E

(b. 1944. D-DAY AND THE LIBERATION OF PARIS)

Founder of Blueprint magazine and New London Architecture,
Murray is an indefatigable promoter of intelligent awareness of architecture.

I LIVE IN BEDFORD PARK IN WEST LONDON, the first garden suburb. Developed in 1875, it was dubbed by John Betjeman the 'most significant suburb in the Western world'. Leading planner Sir Peter Hall used to live here and waxed lyrical about the dendritic plan which drew pedestrians to the local tube station and shops. Most of the amenities locals need are within a nine-minute walk.

Precisely how many minutes works best is open to debate. I've never been very fond of the architecture of Poundbury in Dorset but I love Leon Krier's radical suggestion in his early plans that it should be arranged around principles of the ten-minute town. The Town and Country Planning Association prefers twenty. Carlos Moreno's proposal for *la ville de quart d'heure* has been adopted by Paris Mayor Anne Hidalgo and took the world's urban planners by storm during Covid, which gave suburbs an economic boost but drained the lifeblood from city centres.

Moreno's ideas suit London because of its natural polycentrism, the result of organic growth. Ninety per cent of Londoners live within ten minutes of a high street. At its core, the City of London is still shaped by its mediaeval plan, in spite of the Great Fire and Victorian improvements. Historically, most people there walked, and so they still should.

Pedestrianising the heart of the Square Mile at weekends would help it emerge from its post-pandemic malaise, attracting visitors to its heritage and culture and boosting the bars and restaurants which are dying because of the workers who go in only on Tuesdays, Wednesdays and Thursdays. Unless something is done, the three-day week will destroy the amenities which are essential if the City is to survive as a central business district. It needs more people and a greater mix of uses.

Charles's intervention in the architectural debate in the 1980s began a decade of fruitless style wars, but what emerged from that debate was a consensus that place, the spaces in between, is more important than individual pieces of architecture. Forty years on from his Hampton Court speech when Charles ambushed the architects, it would be great if the revival of the City, and the town centres of his kingdom, became a focus of his reign.

THE PROBLEM WITH OLIGOPOLY

Lord Best O.B.E.

(b. 1945. CLEMENT ATTLEE BECOMES LABOUR PRIME MINISTER)

Social housing expert. One-time President of the Local Government Association.

TODAY'S OLIGOPOLY OF VOLUME HOUSEBUILDERS concentrates on developing new homes on out-of-town, greenfield sites, often with poor access to public transport and green spaces, and with few amenities. There are powerful environmental and social reasons for central and local government, planners and practitioners to pay more attention to keeping and improving our existing housing stock.

Building new homes, however necessary, absorbs irreplaceable land and is hungry for (mostly imported) building materials that contain a great deal of embedded carbon; the construction of new buildings emits more carbon than aviation and shipping combined. Little progress has been made in cutting these emissions. Indeed, an extension of 'permitted development rights' that allows more demolition without planning permission means more buildings being demolished with little regard for whole-life carbon impact. Preserving and upgrading what we have makes sense.

Government funding for modernisation of older stock also offers an opportunity to increase the supply of decent, affordable homes. The private rented sector has the highest proportion of unfit properties. It also has rents that absorb over a third – sometimes more than half – of private tenants' incomes. Yet while the private rented sector has doubled in size this century (to 19% of the stock), the social housing sector has halved (to 17%). We need a rebalancing, with social landlords taking on low quality privately-rented properties and upgrading them.

The time is right for this. With fewer tax incentives and more regulation for private landlords, many are exiting the market. In the 1960s and 1970s, many community-based housing organisations were created to acquire properties from private landlords and then modernise and let them on secure, affordable terms. There is now an ideal opportunity for today's equivalents to go 'back to the future'.

GIVE US BACK OUR STREETS

The Rt. Hon. Lord Waldegrave of North Hill
(b. 1946. MORALE-BOOSTING 'BRITAIN CAN MAKE IT' EXHIBITION AT THE V&A)

Provost of Eton. In 1993, as Science Minister, he offered a prize for the most succinct explanation of the Higgs-Boson phenomenon.

OH TO GET BACK THE CONCEPT OF A STREET and see ancient streets regain their scale. I love good modernist buildings – the taller the better. The Shard's modern-day spire disappearing into the clouds is wonderful. But let's put them together, not scattered everywhere, destroying the scale and the vistas created over centuries. Harold Macmillan's government started the rot, with second-rate high-rises placed at the end of every vista in Hyde Park, spoiling everything from Mayfair to Kensington. We should take all those (not very distinguished) high rises that have been allowed to destroy the backdrop to Westminster and magically group them into new versions of Canary Wharf or La Défense. Actually, add them to Canary Wharf to give that clump the grandeur it doesn't quite achieve.

In the meantime, clear the clutter of signage – now a rural as well as an urban plague – and design what is left with grace. People might even read some of it then. And put up traditional London street signs in the old style on the thousands of corners where we are left baffled in the absence of any names at all.

TOWN TIDYING

Dinah Casson C.B.E.

(b. 1946. JITTERBUG DANCE CRAZE SWEEPS ENGLAND)

Exhibition designer with major projects at The V&A and Imperial War Museum.

I COULD SOUND OFF on how I hate the way that carports (all those grubbed-up privet hedges and flattened walls) have ruined the pleasure of walking along a pavement; or how I detest retro-fitted solar panels and Velux windows, which promise transparency but deliver mirrors. These things batter my enjoyment in walking around towns and cities and I fear no Coronation decorations are going to help me.

Perhaps instead I should return to William Lethaby's rather desperate call in 1916 for a return to town tidying. In an intriguing address to the Arts and Crafts Society, he mourns the separation of art from the ordinary and everyday. In his view, this encourages pundits and performers to work solely for other pundits and performers. He then takes an eyebrow-raising turn, suggesting 'simple, well-off housekeeping in the country, boy-scouting and tennis in flannels' as examples of 'order, construction, beauty, and efficiency' existing in harmony. They represent, he says, 'the best forms of modern civilisation and must serve as examples of the sort of spirit in which town improvement must be undertaken. Everybody must be interested, and it must be half-drill and half-game. I am here to beg you all to play this best of games – town-tidying.'

No doubt his arts and crafts audience nodded more enthusiastically than a contemporary one might (unless our new King was a member of it) but his call to local users to make local decisions is current and desirable. Local isn't always best, or even tidiest, but it *feels* a lot better. Accountability and all that...

TOP OF THE POPS

Piers Gough C.B.E., R.A.

(b. 1946. STEVENAGE CHOSEN AS THE SITE OF THE FIRST 'NEW TOWN')

*Founding Partner of CZWG Architects. An idiosyncratic individualist who
added irreverence and charm to sometimes faddish Post-Modernism.*

ARCHITECTURAL AND PLANNING JOURNOS AND ACADEMICS
love to publish diatribes against the 'privatisation of public space'. These often
imply that existing public spaces such as parks are somehow being stealthily
privatised. This would be shocking if true, but it is not: since at least the 1960s,
local authorities have been increasing public space by pedestrianizing streets and
town centres. So the anti-POPS argument has instead to complain that new
spaces are being provided by developers that look like public space but are still
private; that there is heavy surveillance and that some activities, such as protests,
are forbidden that would be allowed in space owned by a local authority. (But
remember to check those no ball game byelaws first).

But far from being some terrible imposition, these new spaces actually
add to local provision and enrich the tapestry of townscapes. Remember that
up to the 1970s, public access to the Thames or the amazing docks on the Isle
of Dogs and Surrey Quays was blocked by security walls surrounding private
warehouses and sheds. It would have been all too easy to convert those into
gated developments. Instead, there are now continuous paths giving everyone
and his dog access to the river and the docks.

Indeed, the way in which post-war planning policy has allowed local
authorities to insist on public access to private land has been a terrific bonus to
all. New developments of any size are almost always required to provide through-
routes for pedestrians and cycles. The most prevalent recent planning activity
has been demolishing swathes of land-hungry industrial buildings and estates
that were impenetrable or inhospitable and replacing them with housing-led
mixed use projects that offer much more pleasant pedestrian experiences, with
lively frontages and appealing open spaces. Well-known examples are Cabot
Square, Canada Square and Jubilee Park at Canary Wharf, Granary Square and
Coal Drops Yard at King's Cross and now Battersea Power Station. Inaccessible
docks, railway sidings and industrial zones have been transformed into public

space that is inviting, well furnished and cared for, with generous benches, trees and often wonderful play fountains. My unscientific observation is that all sorts of people, including vulnerable minorities, are far more likely to be able to relax and feel safe in such managed environments, partly because developers can usually afford to look after spaces in a way that cash-strapped local authorities struggle to do. The delights usually outweigh the limited constraints on activities that can still perfectly easily be performed elsewhere.

BIBBIDI-BOBBIDI-BOO

Sir Christopher Frayling

(b. 1946. LONDON AIRPORT OPENS)

Vampirologist and Spaghetti Western expert with a masterly overview of Pop Culture. Former Rector of the Royal College of Art.

A MUSIC HALL GAG DOING THE ROUNDS in early summer 1953 went like this:

I've just got a steady job, selling coronation programmes in the Mall.
The pay isn't great, but the hours are terrific!

The hours on 2 June were 10.00–10.40 in the morning and 3.50–4.30 in the afternoon, as the Gold State Coach was pulled by eight grey geldings from Buckingham Palace to Admiralty Arch on its processional route to Westminster Abbey, and—after the three-hour ceremony and lap of honour—back again. The Mall was decorated with banners and four coronet arches, overseen by architect Hugh Casson, fresh from his equivalent role for the Festival of Britain. The BBC— controversially—had an 'observation station' at the Palace end of the Mall and oral histories have confirmed that for the crowds the moment of the Coronation and the glimpse of that Gold Coach had a definite aura about it. Nine English traditions out of ten—including much of the Coronation—dated from the latter part of the nineteenth century, but still it felt ancient. And what's more, it felt like an example of 'order, construction, beauty and efficiency' coming together— Professor W.R. Lethaby's verdict on seeing the Royal Navy in full regalia, in his once-celebrated lecture on 'Town Tidying' (1916).

Meanwhile in 1953, from his base in Burbank California, Walt Disney was commissioning a feasibility study to find the most suitable location for his 'Disneyland': he opted for a site in Anaheim, fed by the expanding Santa Ana freeway. The focal point of this 'theme park' would be Sleeping Beauty Castle, a scaled-down version of Neuschwanstein in Bavaria. Perhaps Disney also had in mind William Randolph Hearst's Castle (1919–1947) in 'the enchanted field' further up the California coast, which had proved for all to see that anyone with a pile of money could become a king.

Fast forward to present-day England, when the whole country has been acquired as a theme park—'the world's leading tourist attraction'—by Walt Disney Enterprises, to amuse and educate American tourists. At least according to Tom Wolfe, who celebrated the year of Orwell's *1984* by writing a predictive fantasy about England in 2020 in which manufacturing has ground to a halt (except for double-decker buses), investment has dried up, productivity has sunk to new lows, and other economies have won the new technology race. Every morning millions of English people, three-quarters of the population, dress up and practise 'dignified servility' as Georgians, Victorians, Bobbies, Guardsmen, Swinging Londoners. A butler nation. Modern buildings have been razed— 'Stirling, Foster, Rogers were never mentioned any longer'—to make way for faux-period architecture with 'antique' finish, much of it designed by Britain's biggest and most prestigious architectural firm Quinlan Terry Associates, though built by a Japanese and Taiwanese workforce ('no one any longer called on Englishmen to do any form of construction at all').

In 1990, Hugh Casson was interviewed by British Library oral history researchers about—among other things—his experience as consultant architect for the Coronation. In retrospect, would he approach the role in the same way as he did in summer 1953? Casson replied that the rise of Disney, and the magic kingdom's fantasy world of heightened royal sumptuousness—imagery which had since gone global—had diminished the impact of real royal trappings, such as the Gold Coach with its eight grey horses. He would now much prefer to see 'a couple of motorbikes and a maroon Rolls-Royce sweep out of Buckingham Palace—it would look more splendid'.

Of course, this was before Rolls-Royce became a wholly-owned subsidiary of the BMW Group (in 2003), and before the outriders' motorbikes became the R1200 TT-P, manufactured by Bayerische Motoren Werke AG—which might have spoilt the symbolism. But the point Casson was making remains a good one. The iconography of the Coronation—the coach and horses leaving the fairytale royal palace—is now in quotation marks. It cannot be real again, and the pageantry now has meaning only as part of an age of lost innocence.

WE'RE THE ONES WHO HAVE TO LOOK AT IT

Valerie Grove

(b. 1946. PUBLICATION OF ORWELL'S *ANIMAL FARM*)

Journalist and literary biographer whose subjects include
John Mortimer and Laurie Lee.

MR. COLLINS WAS A VICTORIAN SPEC BUILDER, responsible for thousands of redbrick villas in North London's metroland. One of them, since 1981, has been ours. The Mr Pooters of the 1890s were proud of their vernacular features: lofty corniced ceilings, pillared porticoes, stained glass, marble fireplaces, Puginesque tiled floors. Having a large family, we needed the space. After stripping the hall wallpaper, we found the pencilled draft of a notice: "This House can be completed in 10 days. Decorations to suit Owner or Tenant. Apply J. Collins, Athenaeum Court, Muswell Hill, N." We chose our Cole & Son wallpapers according to the precise date: 1896.

Sadly, no such respect had been accorded the three detached houses that had stood across the road until 1969. They had been replaced – pre-'Conservation area' – by a high-rise block, Eleanor Rathbone House: flats for sixty-two elderly Jewish refugees.

Miss Eleanor Rathbone, an Independent Labour MP from Liverpool, championed Holocaust survivors. In her name this chimney-like, monolithic, flat-roofed tower of pre-cast concrete panels had risen up while residents watched aghast. Storey piled on storey: twelve in all, obliterating sunlight. Visitors to our house chorused: "Lovely house – ghastly building opposite!" One day in 1987, I heard that its architect was still alive. Walter H. Marmorek, aged 75, from Vienna. He agreed to an interview for my *Sunday Times* column, *à propos* the Prince of Wales's 'monstrous carbuncle' views. He was charming. His office was in Gray's Inn Square, its date etched in stone over his door: 1667. But above his desk was a framed image of his monstrosity, photographed from the south: pristine white, gleaming in sun, amidst trees. Nothing like our rear vision of its damp-stained grey concrete lift-shaft, a blot on our landscape, visible for miles.

Dr. Marmorek had never been back to see his handiwork. "This was how we built in 1969," he shrugged. "High, and economically." It came in within budget (£270,487). Did it please him as much as the 17th century buildings around him now?, I asked. He laughed and said that was a leading question. He even said: "Architects have a disadvantage, compared to doctors. We cannot bury our mistakes." Quite. Reinforced concrete and galvanised steel in inappropriate places can't be forgiven, like a passing ugly fashion: it is unavoidably visible, for all time. I believe that architects' names should be prominently displayed on every building. *Si monumentum requiris, circumspice*, said Christopher Wren. Today, *quis fecit?* we ask, helplessly.

Dr. Marmorek sent me a Christmas card every year thereafter. The residents of his building have died, as has he, aged 100. He was childless but his legacy lingers. This year the current owners, a property firm, are rebuilding the low-rise annexe to his original structure. Our protests to their planning application were fruitless. Two storeys are now five. We watch as another featureless slab blights our life. I echo Robert Byron's words : "Of all the arts, architecture is the nearest to the most people, affects their happiness most closely, obtrudes on their sight most often..."

THE PLAYFUL CAROLEAN CITY

George Ferguson C.B.E.

(b. 1947. INDIAN INDEPENDENCE)

In Bristol in 2012, Ferguson became the first architect to become mayor of a major city. He had already exceeded the limitations of his profession, developing and regenerating Bristol's old Tobacco Factory on his own account.

AS WE ENTER THE ERA OF CHARLES III, the best gift for our children would be greater freedom to play, not in civic playgrounds but within and beyond their communities. Let's liberate our city streets and spaces for those who have had so much exploration and opportunity stolen from them.

The city, never perfect, used to be our playground, and must become so again. We have, throughout the Elizabethan years, slowly filled our streets with vehicles and emptied them of fun. The pushback has started with small offerings, but it seems that the short-term election cycle inhibits politicians from doing what is necessary when faced with the fury of the car lobby.

It is not good enough to condemn our children to spaces left over after planning. For transformative change we need to see our towns and cities from the viewpoint of the child, as advocated by the anarchist architect Colin Ward in his 1977 book, *The Child in the City*. For the sake of their physical and mental health, we should put children at the heart of our urban policymaking, planning with them and for them. Encouraging starts have been made in Bristol, where residential streets have been made safe for children to play in and high streets freed on Sundays for strolling, sitting, dancing and playing. Temporary initiatives like this that allow all to experience the pleasure of traffic-free environments are easily replicable.

As architects, we tend to think in terms of what we can add to spaces to make them more playable, but often the greater need is to remove obstacles. Simply getting rid of the majority of vehicles from city streets and spaces opens them up to a multitude of other uses. For children to play freely they first need to be safe to roam, and to *feel* safe when doing so.

Over the past half-century we have let the car dominate while our Dutch and Danish colleagues have prioritised walking and cycling, creating civilised streets fit for all. As Colin Ward put it, 'a city that is really concerned with the needs of the young will make the whole environment accessible to them'. While we should strive to make our villages, towns and cities more beautiful, while we should protect our historic buildings, spaces and skylines, we must do so in a way that makes them more welcoming.

HOMO ACCOMMODATUS

Ian Ritchie C.B.E., R.A.

(b. 1947. WEDDING OF PRINCESS ELIZABETH AND LT. PHILIP MOUNTBATTEN)

Architect whose buildings include the Reina Sofia Art Museum in Madrid and Bermondsey tube station on the Jubilee Line Extension.

HOMO SAPIENS HAS PROVED LESS THAN WISE. *Homo faber* describes us more accurately, and everything we make is first designed. Humans are unique in the manufactured legacy we leave, including the built environment on which we depend. Yet maintaining this environment requires continual input of resources, whereas the natural world generally sustains itself through cycles of renewal, often with complex interdependencies.

To create a genuinely sustainable human society and its corresponding built environment, we must make a paradigm shift in human behaviour and what we value. We must develop a collectively-held new cognisance. The next step in the evolution of humankind surely needs to be *Homo accommodatus*, attuned to interdependence with each other and the biosphere. Let's hope that future generations will look back positively on this era as one when we learned how to live in harmony.

A starting point might be urban space. Ruskin said that 'the measure of any great civilisation is in its cities and a measure of a city's greatness is to be found in the quality of its public spaces, its parks and squares'. It is therefore a problem that, despite glorious exceptions, our public realm is characterised by shabbiness, inadequate maintenance and a sense of neglect. The flame of civic pride that created Georgian squares and Victorian parks has died to a flickering light. Here and worldwide, the soul of our cities is at stake as we witness the privatisation of urban spaces, a dystopian model of public disenfranchisement.

Charles III has been a radical environmentalist for decades. His Coronation is an ideal opportunity to declare our collective interest in renewing our public urban spaces and to celebrate a creative and enduring sense of community and partnership. It is in this spirit of low-cost, environmentally-intelligent design that I suggest inviting all local authorities in the United Kingdom to commit to creating inclusive, high-quality and atmospheric public space. Municipalities, utility companies and national government could share the funding. Focussing on the preciousness of light and water, the essence of life on earth, it would demonstrate a collective desire for green space and urban beauty.

STOP ALL BUILDING

Jonathan Meades

(b. 1947. THE FIRST EDINBURGH FESTIVAL)

Often dark, sometimes bleak, a believer in lost causes,
Meades is Britain's finest and most controversial architectural writer
since Ian Nairn.

ROBERT BYRON BELONGED TO THE BIOG MOB, that narcissistic gang of brittle inter-war 'well-born', self-proclaimed wits who were not that witty (a Mitford or two, dear Cecil Beaton, the heavily made-up Stephen Tennant, Patrick Leigh Fermor, Lord Berners). His effortully contrary opinions – 'Shakespeare wrote like a grocer' - are simply silly. His Arabism went hand in hand with 'social' anti-semitism. His precious limp-wristed prose might have been designed to demonstrate that the upper classes should be deterred from writing. The same stricture might be applied to the Mob's epigones – Bruce Chatwin *et al.* They may be dead but their shades are self-perpetuating. Their ostentatious good taste has, getting on for a century after their heyday, made the Georgian the referent for 'civilised refinement', 'gracious living', 'decorous comportment' and various other resistible handicaps.

Today the likelihood of an eighteenth century setpiece such as the Adelphi being demolished is all but non-existent. Like politicians, we have 'learned lessons moving forward' into a future that values the past and its artefacts. Or have we? There is a multitude of other targets for the demolition community, which is of course an essential adjunct of the building trade. We may smugly congratulate ourselves on acts of rescue, as though we are loyal St Bernards bearing brandy, but we refuse to recognise that once a building is completed it becomes prey. It may live for decades or centuries. More likely it will be reduced to rubble before its thirtieth birthday at the behest of a stinking rich volume builder and a well-buttered mayor – figures from Dix or Grosz or Rowson. And the more recent the work, the shorter its likely lifespan. Georgian buildings were a soft cause. Victorian ones were harder. The concrete idioms lumped together as brutalism are close to becoming a lost cause, despite a loud reawakening of appreciation of their sculptural sublimity. The new King may loathe their forms and materials but he will surely recognise that they must be preserved as tokens of the era that made them, evidence of an optimism without limits which defined the first and happier half of late Queen's reign.

The gamut of buildings which merit conservation should be extended according to aesthetic worth rather than use or age or association. By that new measure, a 1970s warehouse may well be superior to a 'Waterloo Church' of Georgianism's last gasp. Both can be transformed, 'repurposed'. There is no need to build anew. The new reign's signature should be a ten-year moratorium on building, on a sky crosshatched with cranes, on considerate brickies and traffic chaos. Doing nothing is, as always, a feasible option. Let indigent builders beg in the streets they have sullied with shininess.

CITIES FIT FOR GOSSIP

Peter Rees C.B.E.

(b. 1948. KING CHARLES III BORN)

Professor of Places and City Planning at the Bartlett School of Architecture.
As the City of London's Chief Planning Officer, Rees was closely involved
in the radical evolution of its skyline.

IN 1953, A YOUNG BOY SITS CLOSE to a nine-inch television screen. The parlour behind a Welsh Valley corner shop is packed with neighbours celebrating the Queen's Coronation. In flickering monochrome, I receive my first live images from London and my love affair with this magic city is born. Soon afterwards, a passing express train attracts my attention. Every carriage window frames a lighted table-lamp on a white cloth. I rush home to demand the identity and destination of this train and resolve that one day it will transport me to Paddington. My dream is realised when I begin to study architecture at The Bartlett and become a Londoner.

Mid-twentieth century Britain enjoyed civic pride. Community was a geographically defined concept; gossip was moderated through face-to-face transmission; the workplace and pub were social hubs. We learned the long-trodden shortcuts and loyally supported local trades and services.

The early twenty-first century sees us moving towards a virtual future. Communities are now composed of minoritized groups, linked through social media with its weaponised gossip. Customers in pubs and coffee shops are glued to their iPhones. Train passengers never look out of the window. Pedestrians navigate by screen maps rather than landmarks. Sustainable places cannot be created by planners and architects alone - they must be made by people, with our help. But we are disconnecting from our surroundings and are losing our civic pride.

Town centres are dying and face some difficult planning challenges. Takeaways, bars and hair salons are not enough to create a successful high street. Offices must re-establish their role as social hubs where we mentor the skills of the next generation. Vacant retail space should be repurposed for small businesses, technical education and key social services. Investment apartments may be highly profitable but are under-occupied and create ghost neighbourhoods. We must recreate downtown as a vibrant focus for human contact, gossip and sharing creative ideas.

In 2023, a solitary old man contemplates the skyline from his twenty-seventh floor City apartment. The images are now clear and in full colour. I have enjoyed a life-long love affair with my favourite place, proud to be a Londoner and delighted that my dream came true. No one knows what is next for this amazing metropolis, but London will continue to adapt to every challenge. After all, it has survived two thousand years of plague, fire, war, and planning. 'All change please! Mind the gap!'

BUILD IT AGAIN, SAM

Brian Hatton

(b. 1948. NATIONAL HEALTH SERVICE FOUNDED)

A senior figure in Liverpool's School of Art and Design, Hatton writes with passion about the fascination and disturbing character of this unique city.

IT'S ODD THAT, WHILE SONGS AND PLAYS ARE RE-PERFORMED, buildings are built but once and, when demolished, are almost never rebuilt. Odd, too, that while conservatories train music students to be performers or conductors, architecture schools proceed as if their graduates will be composers. Yet when Goethe described architecture as 'frozen music', he meant music performed and heard. Might it help the cause of architectural conservation if architecture schools became conservatories: design understood less as composing than as performing, and buildings regarded as iterated performances like those described in George Kubler's great rethinking of art history, *The Shape of Time*?

It might be countered that this is implicit in building typology, that classical architecture is based in reiteration of the Orders. That is true, but what today could be the model of a column? Adolf Loos, in proposing a Doric column for the Chicago Tribune, implied that it was the high-rise itself. So, just as Doric columns were built again and again, why not entire buildings and ensembles? And if fine buildings are demolished, why not build them again? If listed buildings are demolished even with permits, might we require the developers to recreate them elsewhere? That would make them think twice. We have to kick the juvenile futurist habit of novelty without limit. For what is architecture but limits defined with wisdom, and refined with grace?

There are many ways of reiterating, from detailed design to whole districts, from literal to poetic. Seeking to recover continuity after war, division and abruption, the International Building Exhibition in Berlin in 1987 upgraded Kreuzberg's dense blocks through 'Cautious Urban Renewal', while Friedrichstadt's razed eighteenth century grid was restocked according to a policy of 'Critical Reconstruction'. Note the word 'critical': ignored, alas, in the recent dumb resurrection of Berlin's Royal Palace. Psychological as well as practical necessity calls for reconstruction rather than resurrection. And even where reconstruction can't be done, an unforgotten place may be remembered elsewhere, as with Stirling's Stuttgart gallery courtyard. That circle of fragments traced, I think, the drum beneath the dome of Liverpool's enormous neoclassic Custom House, revealed to the sky by German bombs in 1941 and recalled from Stirling's Liverpool youth.

MORE DELICACY

Duncan Fallowell

(b. 1948. MAHATMA GANDHI MURDERED)

Aesthete, punk champion, essayist, librettist and award-winning travel-writer, Fallowell combines a radical sensibility with profound respect for established values.

EVERYWHERE IN THE WORLD, DELICACY IS VANISHING. Corporations and committees hate it. It gets in the way. Let us try to keep such delicacy as remains.

At Oxford, I had rooms on Folly Bridge, an island of Regency delicacy in the middle of the Isis. Our house had a walled garden with pear trees. It was purchased by Pembroke College, who replaced the garden with an unwalled tarmac car-park.

English Heritage has repainted the library at Kenwood in Las Vegas white, blue, pink. Their brochure reprints Adam's original superb colour scheme. On a visit to Holkham Hall to view the classical sculpture, I was halted by a vast garish crimson carpet installed in the gallery, rendering the statues invisible. Clandon Park near Guildford was gutted by fire in 2015. The National Trust received £63 million insurance to restore it. The state rooms were among the greatest works of Italian *stuccatori* in Britain. The Trust said it would not restore them because the skills no longer existed. Untrue, but it amounts to an official statement that restoration requiring delicacy will not be undertaken.

Even enlightened local authorities have a hard time retaining delicacy. Westminster approved a recent renovation of the Burlington Arcade that involved the removal of the central lanterns. I protested. They showed me pre-renovation photographs: no central lanterns. Alas, they were using 1950s photos; the lanterns had been beautifully restored since then. The planning department had not visited the site. Westminster admitted its mistake.

Streets, trees, good lighting are essential to civilised townscape. 'New' need not be indelicate; but developers hate streets, love huge lumps. The makeover of Trafalgar Square suffers greatly from the elimination of the square's trees. I proposed improving the crude lighting in Belgrave Square - the authorities said no, it was primarily a traffic island.

I once wrote to Buckingham Palace asking if they would restore the Nash trophies and statues on the skyline. The clerk of works wrote back that they were in Coade stone, cracking, and taken down for safety. No plans to restore them. What a wonderful act of finesse if our new Sovereign were to do so, so that the garden front looked not like a town hall but like a palace.

Stop urban crudeness spreading into the delicate countryside (giant prefab sheds, enforced housing quotas, polytunnels etc). Stop clearance for prairie farming. The progressive elimination of delicacy leads only to one end: desolation.

A TAX ON GUM AND A CLUTTER CULL

Michael Morrison

(b. 1948. LAND-ROVER LAUNCHED AT AMSTERDAM MOTOR SHOW)

Senior Partner at Purcell, the world's largest firm of conservation architects.

HOW HORRID CHEWING GUM IS! Much of my working life has been spent in museums and galleries, churches and other buildings open to the public, and I have been appalled by the way that discarded gum disfigures new stone pavements, gets stuck under seats and pews or is spat into the most inappropriate places. It is so very difficult to remove. Banning manufacture and sale of chewing gum, Singapore-style, ought to be a political priority. As an interim measure, perhaps we could have a £5 tax on every packet of gum, to be allocated to cleaning up the wretched stuff.

My next obsession is the clutter of signs in our streets: pavements blocked with sandwich boards, adverts strapped to railings and a plethora of signs put up by local authorities to control traffic. Driving into Norwich recently, I counted thirty-five traffic signs in a 350-yard stretch of road – far too many signs to read at 30mph. My mind turned to my Norfolk village, population 2,500, situated where two B-roads cross. Here, it turns out, we have 293 signs, not even counting milestones or signs for street names, bus stops and footpaths. There are eighty-four signs setting the speed limit, five solar-powered electric machines that flash to tell you to slow down and an additional eighty-five general traffic signs. In the village centre, I counted thirty-one advertisements that were either freestanding or attached to fences. And I gave up counting the multitude of *ad hoc* signs stuck to lamp posts, mostly telling you not to let your dog foul the pavement. The local highway authority could save a small fortune by rationalising this signage. If the village had a single 20mph limit, fourteen posts with two signs each would do the job and most of the remaining fifty-eight signs could be removed. Calmness would descend in place of a jarring, confusing mess.

HAVE MORE FUN

Robert Adam

(b. 1948. RAILWAYS NATIONALISED)

The most provocative of the new classical architects, a tireless advocate of traditional design and an unapologetic critic of modernism.

WE ALL LIKE PLACES TO BE INTERESTING AND INDIVIDUAL. We look for landmarks. We notice features and decoration. We call it 'character'. And we don't want everything to be the same.

Architects and designers, however, don't want their precious façades messed up. Decoration is suspicious and little features are ridiculed as 'gob-ons'. The design police (public and private) go for bland and unobtrusive additions. They get upset if people paint their houses the 'wrong' colour. Individual expression or 'personalisation' comes close to a crime. The irony is that this is exactly what architects do. They want people to recognise a design as specifically theirs. But this isn't allowed for *hoi polloi*, the people who will live there.

If the place is historic, there are laws to stop you changing things. Most of those places aren't the Royal Crescent. Their charm mostly comes from the personalisation, odd features and quirks that designers and owners have put on, often over centuries. But the moment it was decided that it was historic, all that had to stop. The place changes from being a pulsing, living organism to being museum-piece taxidermy, controlled by powerful curators. Character becomes what it is, not what it might be.

Why is it that older places, even those just a few decades old, often feel better than when they were first built and the architects took their publicity photos? It's because people have made them into home. They've gone beyond show homes or up-for-rent offices. Like worn-in shoes, they're more comfortable and they're individual. Big changes are often made: some buildings come down, others are added. Little changes are made: porches and extensions are added, windows are repainted or replaced, front gardens all become different, signs and names are put up. To those with superior judgement, some of this may be a sin against good taste. But who is it all for? We know some of the quirks of the past were sins to our sophisticated forebears, but still we preserve them.

Taste wardens should back off. Just set a few simple rules – or codes – for what happens after a place is built: things like maximum height, size of extensions, how far the front can project, but not much more. You need to protect neighbours from encroachment, not other people's taste. People should have more fun with their buildings.

UNFASTEN YOUR GREEN BELT

Peter Studdert

(b. 1949. NATO FOUNDED)

Independent adviser on city planning and design.

GREEN BELTS ARE RIGHTLY SEEN as one of the jewels in the crown of post-war planning policy in the UK. Since their introduction in the 1950s, they have prevented our major cities from sprawling into the countryside and have promoted compact settlements. They have also encouraged the regeneration of brownfield land in cities. Although many people still see them as sacrosanct, others see them as promoting unsustainable patterns of development by dispersing development beyond the Green Belt and encouraging overdevelopment of the few remaining brownfield sites within cities. More and more, Green Belts are seen as one of the main impediments to addressing the housing crisis. Is it time for a more nuanced approach?

It should be remembered that the Green Belt is a planning rather than a landscape designation: its primary purpose is to prevent sprawl and help safeguard the countryside from encroachment. It does not explicitly promote access to the countryside for city dwellers. But in exceptional cases where land is removed from the Green Belt for development, the National Planning Policy Framework encourages 'compensatory improvements to the environmental quality and accessibility of remaining Green Belt land'.

Surely this indicates where future Green Belt policy should lie: providing recreation and leisure for city dwellers. Development should be encouraged on low amenity land close to public transport corridors, so long as it is paired with nearby high amenity land that would be held in trust and made accessible for public enjoyment. In view of the uplift in land value that would flow from the Green Belt release, each acre of development land should protect and enhance at least ten acres of high amenity value land, together with an endowment for its future management. Over time, the Green Belt would develop into a Green Wheel, with 'spokes' of new development along public transport corridors radiating from the city and separated by high value protected landscape managed for the benefit of city dwellers: a Green Belt fit for the twenty-first century.

INVEST IN PUBLIC SPACE

Loyd Grossman C.B.E.

(b. 1950. STONE OF SCONE STOLEN FROM WESTMINSTER ABBEY)

Rock musician, restaurant critic, art historian,
Chairman of The Royal Parks.

A NATIONAL COMMITMENT to the improvement and expansion of the public realm would be an appropriate way to celebrate the coronation of our new King. In a society obsessed with egotism and financial reward, space is everywhere under threat of being privatised and monetised.

The experience of the pandemic has shown us how important public space is. Our parks made a huge contribution to improving our physical and spiritual health and an even greater contribution to social cohesion and a sense of community: together with other public spaces, they are among the few places which show that we are 'all in this together'. But local authority budgets for the care of parks seem to be in a perpetual state of crisis. Although we are the sixth richest country in the world, too many towns and cities feel shabby, uncared for and neglected. Putting more energy, more creative thought and of course more money – some of which should come from the private sector – into our parks, squares and shared townscape could go a long way towards restoring our recently battered national pride and self-confidence.

REDRESSING DISTRESSING WINDOWS

Theo Fennell

(b. 1951. THE TERM 'ROCK'N'ROLL' COINED BY AN AMERICAN 'DISC JOCKEY')

Rock-star jewellery designer with a stellar list of celebrity clients.

WINDOW SHOPPING IS ONE of the most innocent and pleasurable ways to spend those rescued moments in a throbbing metropolis, or even a quiet provincial town. It allows our Walter Mitty daydreams to have a little substance.

Some places are a delight to browse. The raucousness of Carnaby Street and the gentility of Jermyn Street are wonderful. What they have in common is character, a lack of ubiquitous branding and often a sensitive use of light: excessive lighting that bleaches out architecture, history and design is one of the most grating aspects of shopping streets today.

The window displays themselves are the work of a merchandiser whose taste and innovation we cannot control. But the frames of the windows, the façades and the signage around them are things that can and should be controlled for the greater good. Ideally, a relaxed but aesthetically gifted group of people would look at improving what is already there and sign off on any new presentation. These arbiters need some real talent, experience and understanding so they can suggest improvements as well as judge what needs to be changed. They should have deep empathy with and love of the urban landscape.

The result would not be bland homogeneity. A certain vulgarity or crassness can suit the surroundings and a monochromatic scheme can sit well with the elegance of its neighbours. The aim would be frontages and signage that embellish the neighbourhood while suiting the local ambience. Where this happens, it is nearly always successful in bringing people to the area. Where it doesn't, we should shame the perpetrators and hold a competition to suggest the best, Gilbertian punishment for unpleasant frontages – perhaps two days and nights in their own window for those responsible, under a flashing sign saying 'I did this'.

LET'S ALL BE DESIGN CRITICS

Stephen Bayley

(b. 1951. THE FESTIVAL OF BRITAIN)

Author and critic. Founding Director of The Design Museum.
Chairman of The Royal Fine Art Commission Trust.

WE KNOW THAT GOD LAUGHS AT OUR PLANS. Especially Masterplans. Yet we're told Masterplans will save our cities from messy chaos. But I like shabby wabi sabi. I like Soane's hazard and surprise. I admire the grandeur of Robert Moses, but prefer the charm of Jane Jacobs. Never forget the role of accidents and mistakes in creating beauty. Masterplans smell too much of Soviet autocracy, a rule by numbers and scale: Stalin knew that quantity has a quality all its own. The Masterplan is bureaucracy's heartless attack on individuality. Show me one that works.

We agree that no-one wants to live in an ugly city. How to make things better? Wait a minute, because wisdom is not knowing what to do, but what to do *next*. There are quick fixes for urban malaise: cruel and unusual punishments for people who drop litter; guerrilla gardening to be valorised, not penalised; a requirement for residents to clean the streets in front of their properties; urban wastes to be afforested; severe fines for incompetently managed utilities contracts. But these are details. What's needed is something more abstract: a larger change of behaviour, a democracy of higher expectations where everyone is judge and jury of their surroundings, not a victim of them. Apathy is its own punishment. But, additionally, apathy leads to urban misery.

You can't legislate for taste and charm. To do so would drain enchantment from the world: legislation has limitations. But I'd nonetheless want to establish a national art school where attendance was compulsory and we spoke about aesthetics as we speak about the weather. Attendees, which means all of us, would learn to interrogate their cities, putting architects, planners, officials, developers and politicians under pitiless scrutiny. Everyone would be a design critic, always demanding 'Is this really the best you can do?'

Behaviour can change quickly. Drunk driving is stigmatised, smoking marginalised, simian groping criminalised. Legislation helped, but it was supported by popular consent, a change of mood about intolerable conduct that was undetected until it was upon us. Why tolerate ugliness and squalor?

The sacred mystery of any great city is this: unconscious agreement by citizens and visitors that it's where you want to be. It wasn't a Masterplan with its spurious clarity that created this yes-effect. It was individual activity.

I'd like to stop God howling with derision and let Him smile in gentle approval.

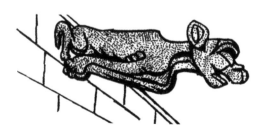

TURN DOWN THE LIGHTS

Alex Lifschutz

(b. 1952. GREAT SMOG OF LONDON)

A psychologist as well as an inspired designer. Projects include the Golden Jubilee Bridges and Broadwall social housing on the South Bank.

WHAT ONE THING COULD WE DO IN OUR CITIES that, at a stroke, would save energy, carbon and money? That would show we cherish our birds, insects, all our urban ecology? That would help ease the climate emergency, create beauty and restore our awe at the stars in the night sky? It's extraordinarily simple. Turn down the lights.

Millions of people use streets and public spaces after dark, yet the garish splash of unnecessary illumination gives them neither safe public lighting nor places of beauty. Sensitively-lit public spaces come last behind a free-for-all of dazzling shops and deserted offices, crass illuminated advertising and artless highway lighting that obliterates the night sky, diminishes our fauna and makes places we enjoy in the daytime trashy and trivial.

At the same time, our cities are full of public landmarks, beautiful monuments and great architecture that languish unlit or ill-lit like St Paul's Cathedral, unable to contribute to the poetry of the night-time city or act as landmarks to guide us. They don't need to be spotlit. An office desk is lit at 400 lux, a suburban street at 30 lux: our eyes adapt, and subtle lighting is more congenial and efficient than the glaring light around most office blocks. Just by turning down unnecessary lights, the perception of landmarks and public spaces will automatically improve. Adding inexpensive, subtly-accented lighting to our great architecture would transform our cities at night into places that are the equal of the daytime scenes that make the United Kingdom one of the world's most visited places.

Light pollution is as undesirable as any other kind and as easily discouraged by regulation and taxes. It's time to reimagine our cities and the landmarks we use to navigate them, just as in 1669, in the reign of an earlier King Charles, Wren reimagined London after the Great Fire.

RETHINKING REGENERATION

Sir Howard Bernstein

(b. 1953. ASCENT OF EVEREST BY HILLARY AND TENZING)

As Chief Executive of Manchester City Council and Manchester Millennium Ltd, orchestrator the city's spectacular renaissance after the 1996 terrorist bomb.

SINCE 1953, OUR TOWNS AND CITIES have shown they can reinvent themselves and prosper anew in the face of significant change. Take East Manchester: once the powerhouse of the Industrial Revolution, its economy collapsed in the 1970s and 1980s as globalisation changed trade patterns, leaving behind industrial dereliction and deprivation. A sustained effort has enabled it to recover to the point where it now offers globally-competitive sports, leisure and entertainment facilities.

There are other such success stories, but we need to focus on how urban renewal creates opportunities in a world reshaped by climate, social, digital and economic change, a world in which factors beyond geographic boundaries shape the fortunes of even the smallest place. It is, frankly, a failure if not everyone can benefit from urban renewal. Doing it successfully means housing options that enable people to stay in their communities through their lives, homes that are built with climate imperatives and income disparities in mind. It means reclaiming space from cars and promoting shared mobility and accessible travel. And it means planning communities in a way that reduces inequality and creates opportunities for new generations with new needs and new priorities. The industries of old, by and large, will not return, but there is much opportunity if we create spaces for ideas and emerging industries to thrive.

Delivery mechanisms also need updating, with an end to piecemeal development and value extraction. For regeneration to be truly sustainable, every community should have a regeneration framework built on the needs and opportunities of its current and future residents.

A FESTIVAL OF AFFORDABLE HOUSING

John McAslan C.B.E.

(b. 1954. WARTIME RATIONING FINALLY ENDS)

Prolific architect with a special interest in integrating new with old, notably at King's Cross Station, The Roundhouse and Peter Jones in Sloane Square.

BRITAIN HAS SOME OF THE WORLD'S FINEST ARCHITECTS, engineers and creative energy: a community of makers able to mobilise to put public housing at the top of their agendas. To mark the Coronation of His Majesty the King, I propose a national housing plan that seeks to resolve, once and for all, Britain's affordable and homeless housing crisis. In parallel, as an expression of commitment, a Festival of Affordable Housing should be inaugurated with an ambition to match the aspirations and long-term positive outcomes of the 1951 Festival of Britain.

Such initiatives are urgently needed. It's alarming to think that, in 2023, almost ten million people in the United Kingdom, including three and a half million children, live in sub-standard housing. One and a half million households are on social housing waiting lists as successive governments fail to meet affordable housebuilding targets (currently set at 300,000 housing units a year). As a result, more and more households are pushed into the unstable private rented sector.

The statistics for homelessness are equally grim: the UK's 100,000 homeless households (including 120,000 children) live in the most sub-standard of temporary accommodation. A further 500,000 are regarded as being part of the constituency of 'hidden homeless'. Beyond this, rough sleepers spend a total of one million nights a year living on the streets. Those who are homeless suffer low life expectancies and long-term physical and mental health problems, placing a significant additional burden on the NHS. In monetary terms alone, homelessness creates a UK government obligation in the region of £3 billion annually. In short, the UK has a shameful record of failing to build enough good quality, low-cost affordable homes and decent long-term accommodation for the homeless.

Action is required now to address this. Government must lead by empowering local authorities, developers, housebuilders (who dominate the provision of new homes) and social housing providers to transform the environment within which affordable housing is built and targets met, whilst enabling some long-term homeless accommodation to be embedded in residential-led, mixed-use developments that are high-quality and sustainable.

Crucially, the UK government and construction industry must embrace and invest in Modern Methods of Construction in order to provide, from centres across the country, the expertise to deliver low carbon new-build and retrofit homes, both on existing sites and on additional land made available for development.

LIVING AND BREATHING

Kim Wilkie

(b. 1955. BBC TELEVISION NEWSREADERS APPEAR FOR THE FIRST TIME)

Landscape designer whose projects range from the influential
Thames Landscape Strategy to Orpheus, an inverted earthen pyramid
for the Duke of Buccleuch at Boughton in Northamptonshire.

OUR INSTAGRAM AGE has become so infatuated with the visual that we are forgetting our other senses. What is the smell and taste of the air? How does our skin feel? Do we hear traffic or birdsong? Architects are encouraged to focus on what buildings look like, rather than examining where and how structures sit on the land and respond to the human and natural context. Is it comfortable? Does it feel right? Or is it just pretty?

Buildings come and go, but the spaces around which they sit last for centuries. St James's Square in London is a good example. Since the 1660s at least, a quarter of its buildings have been replaced every fifty years, and to this day construction never stops; but the open space has held fast and defines the urban pattern. Public spaces determine how we live and breathe. They are the soft suspension that protects us from the rickety ride of urban development. Good urban spaces do lots of things simultaneously. They not only create places to gather and play, but absorb water, clean the air, cool the microclimate and welcome wildlife. The soil and microbial life under the ground is as important as the greenery above.

In new settlements, this should be the starting point: understanding the topography and hydrology; embracing the human and natural history;

following the patterns of movement; then setting out the framework of open space, water and pedestrian connections, before fitting the buildings and streets around it. Obsession with appearance has led to design codes that mandate solutions rather than concentrating on briefs that explore these issues. Briefs and guidance are harder work but they are much better at concentrating on specific sites and a local concept of place. And local communities are far more astute than most developers think. No one likes the idea of concreting over their view, but discussions about houses that their children can afford, and which are set out in a way that respects the land and environment, can begin to make a difference. That does not mean a score card of newts, bats and dormice, nor a codification of façades. Intelligent consultation can draw out the local history, where land floods or freezes, how favourite walks can be connected, whether the local surgeries and schools work. Then a plan based on place and open space emerges. Topography and the movement of water, wildlife and people is what makes cities work.

LEARNING FROM THE PAST

The Duke of Richmond

(b. 1955. SIR WINSTON CHURCHILL RESIGNS AS PRIME MINISTER)

Custodian of the Goodwood Estate, home of the world's best classic car events.

OVER CENTURIES OF SLOW AND ORGANIC GROWTH, our historic towns and cathedral cities have become lovely places to live and work. Because of that, they are required to accept far higher housing allocations than they can manage. Large greenfield housing development is often seen as the only way of achieving the numbers, meaning that the unique form and built environment of historic towns and cathedral cities is threatened by excessive, inappropriate and insensitive housing growth. Instead of beseiging these places, we should learn from them. Often they provide excellent models of sustainable living while managing to conserve their historic legacy.

Conservation and development, far from being mutually exclusive, must go hand-in-hand, with both playing an important part in a broader national and strategic context. That context must reflect several things: the need to build at higher densities in order to conserve greenfield sites and produce compact and sustainable urban areas; the location of major brownfield sites in urban areas; levels of national investment in transport and infrastructure and the growth it will generate; locations where growth can contribute to urban areas; the need for new developments to provide a full range of land uses and reduce the need for commuting; the need to protect productive farmland and food production; the desirability of a 'build it or lose it' condition attached to planning consent. On top of all that, we need new cross-boundary delivery mechanisms and organisations that can assemble land, speed up procedures and ensure high-quality and genuinely sustainable development. A key part of this is to ensure that increases in land value resulting from planning approvals are used to fund infrastructure and community needs.

We can do better in looking after and conserving what we have, better in creating a future environment that will enhance people's lives. But this will never happen with the current lack of vision and innovation in determining the future of housing and development. We are all responsible for that.

THE CASH VALUE OF HERITAGE

Sir Laurie Magnus BT., C.B.E.

(b. 1955. STIRLING MOSS WINS HIS FIRST GRAND PRIX)

Financier and Government adviser responsible for the reorganisation of English Heritage. He is currently Chairman of Historic England.

RESPECT FOR ENGLAND'S ARCHITECTURAL HERITAGE reached a depressing low during the second Elizabethan era. Wrecking balls destroyed countless country mansions, industrial buildings and town houses, erasing the work of brilliant architects and removing a legacy that inspired pride and joy.

The word 'heritage' was dropped from the nomenclature of government because it was perceived to represent a throwback to a world of aesthete-reactionaries who romanticise the past. The Department for Culture, Media and Sport, however wonderful its ministers and staff, strikes only marginal resonance on the streets of Britain. Ask a random sample of a thousand people what matters to them and the answers, evidenced from recent opinion surveys, would show heritage well ahead of culture, media and sport.

But the pendulum is swinging back. In this Coronation year, DCMS has a Minister with 'Heritage' on his door. Heritage Capital is recognised, like Natural Capital, as an essential component when measuring socio-economic wellbeing. Quality of life - mental health, community cohesion and happiness – is seen to benefit from living and working in beautiful places with roots in history and unique architectural features. The fallacy that heritage only involves tourist attractions has been jettisoned as planners accept that it involves the entire historic landscape, including places of worship, archaeological remains and local histories.

Heritage makes a vital contribution to a local sense of pride in place. This, in turn, is a vital catalyst for successful regeneration. Simple measures, such as restoring original high street shop fronts, removing garish signage and engaging school children in researching local historic events, can release a virtuous spiral of revival, with places becoming 'magnets' where people want to live, work and invest.

Heritage is a force for good: a focus for action in repairing left-behind places, a brake (through intelligent retrofitting) on damaging carbon emissions and a source of pride and unity for a great nation. God save the King: and may his ministers restore the mighty "H" currently missing from the DCMS name.

DICTATING TO DEVELOPERS

James Stourton

(b. 1956. BIRTH OF POP ART AT WHITECHAPEL GALLERY)

Biographer of Lord Clark of 'Civilisation' and one-time Chairman of Sotheby's. An influential and respected voice in the heritage world.

I HAVE BEEN GIVEN PLENIPOTENTIARY POWERS to do what I like. Let's start with London. Having nicely re-arranged Trafalgar Square, we move to two areas now crying out for attention: Hyde Park Corner and Marble Arch. Can we have a competition for a plan to improve their composition? The problems can be partly solved with tree planting. A noble row of chestnut trees? And (not strictly architectural but important for the capital) can we do something about Leicester Square, the most dismal of our great squares?

I would uncouple Tate Britain from Tate Modern and give it the independent trustee board it desperately needs to forge its own identity. This older sister presently resembles granny in a miniskirt and pleases nobody. A plea, too, to stop low-grade commemorative sculpture ruining parks and public places. This is what The Royal Fine Art Commission was originally set up for.

Outside the capital, I would concentrate on two areas with a similar root problem, housing and Conservation Areas. Housing, both quality and type, is the great planning issue of our time. We can do it well: look at Accordia and Marmalade Lane in Cambridge, Goldsmith Road in Norwich, and Derwenthorpe near York. But the system has tilted too far towards the interests of the developer. Let's go for the German and Dutch model, where during the development process the land is taken into public control, with a planning office (a vast improvement on what we have over here) dictating to the developer what is wanted and needed.

Conservation Areas are barely worth having unless there is an effective Civic Trust, which is true in only about one in ten cases. Do we care about them or not? If we do, then let our new improved planning office protect them before every suburb is spoiled.

ANTIDOTE TO TERMINAL BOREDOM

Craig Brown

(b. 1957. USSR LAUNCHES SPUTNIK I, THE FIRST ARTIFICIAL EARTH SATELLITE)

Parodist and critic who combines searing wit with acidulous observation. His books include superbly irreverent reveries on The Beatles and Princess Margaret.

YOU ARE ADVISED TO ARRIVE AT THE AIRPORT three hours before departure on international flights, or two hours before for European flights, even if it's only London to Edinburgh. That's two or three hours of boredom punctuated by sudden bursts of panic. The soulless diversions - Banana Republic, Harrods, Marks and Spencer - serve only to increase your sense of twitchiness. When your bags are already full to bursting, why go shopping in an airport? It's as fruitless and dispiriting an activity as going fishing in a carpark, or bungee-jumping in a bungalow.

All that space, all that time, and nothing to fill them with. On the other hand, our national museums are faced with the opposite problem: too little space, too much to put in it. The British Museum currently holds about two million items in storage, and the V&A holds over 250,000. At any one time, the Tate displays only one-fifth of its collection. Everything else is tucked away in the dark.

These are not second-rate works, either. Take one of my favourite British artists, David Jones. Tate Britain holds twenty-seven of his drawings and paintings, many of them given in memory of loved ones, but only two or three are ever on display. Ditto Stanley Spencer, only more so: The Tate holds 237 of his works but most of them can be seen only by appointment. Over the years, Adman's art, oligart - big, bold, brash, ploddingly literal, as accessible as a slogan - has tended to elbow anything more thoughtful and timeless and beautiful out of the way, and into storage.

Two problems: on the one hand, millions of people in airports, ready for the solace of art; on the other, hundreds of thousands of works of art, stored out of view. And one simple solution: as they do at Schiphol, turn departure lounges into galleries, hung with the neglected treasures of our national galleries. If this is a success, the transformation can be repeated elsewhere in the airport. The stress and tedium of snaking towards passport control would be relieved in an instant with the addition of art along the way, showing residents and visitors alike the artistic glories of the country they are about to enter. Bridget Riley, not Banana Republic. Hogarth, not Harrods. Stanley Spencer, not Marks and Spencer. We have nothing to lose but our chain stores.

INSULATE HOUSES WITH WOOL

Sir Nicholas Coleridge C.B.E.

(b. 1957. PUBLICATION OF JACK KEROUAC'S *ON THE ROAD*)

Former publisher of Vogue, Tatler, and Vanity Fair,
now Chairman of the V&A.

IF I COULD CHANGE ONE THING ARCHITECTURALLY in the Carolean Age, it would be the insulation of buildings. Until the Prince of Wales (as he then was) asked me to chair his Campaign for Wool, I had given no thought to insulation. I knew that builders put some sort of padding in the cavities between walls, but that was it.

His Majesty argued, with great passion, that the world was insane not to use more wool. It was natural, sustainable, biodegradable, grew for free on the backs of sheep; so why were we spurning it in favour of oil-based synthetics? Why were we using plastics, nylons and polypropylene for everything, when they will linger in landfill for centuries, perhaps forever? Wool made sense for clothing, made sense for carpets. And it made sense for insulation, said the King.

Virtually every one of the near-identical new build houses that slowly engulf our countryside year by year has walls filled with synthetic insulation. The builders consider no other solution; it is either plastic-cased blocks or synthetic foam, pumped into the cavities for warmth. Yet low-grade wool is far more effective, holds heat better, and acts as a coolant in hot weather. For various reasons, the volume housebuilders have resisted using wool. I know, as I wrote to a lot of them on behalf of the King. They said there wasn't enough wool to go round (incorrect); that the thickness of wool insulation would make rooms in new houses smaller (surely not); that wool attracts moths (not if sprayed). The real reason, of course, is that it is simpler to pump walls with synthetics and that wool insulation is slightly more expensive. Wool has, however, never been cheaper; a shocking amount of it is thrown away or burnt by farmers every year as the price is so low.

Wouldn't it be glorious, as a new King takes the throne – a King with greater environmental credentials than any previous Monarch, greater than almost anyone else alive – if the housebuilders converted to wool? As they roll out their identikit houses, might they not stop and reflect that to do so would be the greatest gift they could give the King, and the nation; a gift for which they would be applauded forever and ever.

WAYS OF NOT SEEING

David Jenkins

(b. 1957. ELVIS PRESLEY RELEASES 'ALL SHOOK UP')

An architect by training who turned to high-concept publishing, creating some of Phaidon's finest architecture and design books.

AS LIFE-LONG STUDENTS OF ARCHITECTURE, we contemplate Lutyens' government buildings in New Delhi and admire his erudition. Or look up at the Seagram Building, in New York, and marvel at Mies's sense of harmony. Or study Le Corbusier's Parisian villas and enjoy the concise language of Purism. Or do we? What if, instead, we see only symbols of oppressive colonialism, corporate exploitation, and white male privilege?

In *Ways of Seeing* (1972), John Berger observed that our reading of an image or artefact is determined by what we know, and that any such reading may evolve over time. Each generation introduces different perceptions and new cultural imperatives. The Academy evolves. The gaze changes. But how do we see if we know nothing? Or worse, if we regard history as suspect, and education as a corrupting influence: if we reject everything?

The early Modernists were schooled in the Beaux Arts tradition. They drew from a vast body of knowledge, and an intellectual and cultural heritage dating back centuries. They chose to reject much of it, but they also made connections. One can imagine Ictinus happily thumbing through *Vers une architecture* or Callicrates commending the Modulor. Succeeding generations were similarly grounded. And there were great historians too, inspirational figures who brought architectural history vividly to life. Vincent Scully was an iconic presence at Yale, as was Reyner Banham at the Bartlett, and Joseph Rykwert at Pennsylvania. As Philip Johnson observed, you cannot not know history.

But the landscape is changing. We live in an age of sampling, collaging and cut-and-paste. It becomes a problem when architecture students rank Kanye West above Alvar Aalto or Louis Kahn, when they never open a book or visit a library, when their preferred optic is the iPhone. What happens when non-art-historical critiques are applied to architecture, thus obstructing any meaningful engagement; when nobody wants to talk about the canon; and when the historian is ultimately unwelcome?

In many schools, history and theory programmes are disappearing altogether. Lectures are no longer given. Collective memories are lapsing or being erased. Increasingly, students are being left to explore their own experiences. To translate their own instincts and neuroses into built form. As if design skills are somehow immanent and study unnecessary. We are approaching educational ground zero. Contemplate the future of architecture and despair.

PAINT THE TOWN RED

Hanif Kara O.B.E.

(b. 1958. LONDON'S FIRST PARKING METER INSTALLED)

Structural engineer and Professor of Practice in Architectural Technology at Harvard Graduate School of Design.

DESPITE ALL ITS GLORY, London could be still more colourful. Colour is an essential part of our daily lives; it can have a profound impact on our emotions, moods and perceptions. Central London is a perfect example of how colour can conjure unique emotions. From bright red telephone boxes and the famous red buses to black cabs, it has a palette that is iconic and instantly recognisable.

It's not just landmarks that are steeped in colour. Ceremonial events, such as the Changing of the Guard at Buckingham Palace, with soldiers dressed in bright red uniforms and bearskins, add to the gaiety. The Pride parade, where participants don rainbow-coloured costumes, is a kaleidoscopic celebration of diversity. Streets and neighbourhoods such as Notting Hill and Southall are filled with a rainbow of hues, while markets, as in Borough and Camden, are an explosion of colour where stalls sell everything from fresh produce to handmade crafts in a spectrum of shades. Street art also adds colour, with vibrant murals enlivening Shoreditch, Hackney and other areas.

We can expand this to the rest of London by investing in colour across all thirty-three boroughs, so lifting the mood of the people, leaving a lasting impression on visitors and having a positive impact on the next generation. The Coronation can be a decisive trigger, above the confines of regulation and politics, for recalibrating and reinventing our building stock in this way, without demonising new buildings or architecture itself.

WHITE WATER CITY

Geoffrey Matthews

(b. 1959. c.p. snow's *two cultures* published)

Former soldier, now Secretary of The Chelsea Arts Club.

THERE'S A JOY IN TRAFFIC – or at least in navigating it. I love driving in London. In part it's that I like knowing my way around: I've been navigating the city's roads for nearly fifty years and whilst some of my favourite shortcuts have been closed off there are still some that give me a real sense of satisfaction. My favourite route from the National Portrait Gallery to the Mirror building on Holborn (via Maiden Lane, Great Queen Street and Bream's Buildings) doesn't work any more, but I still like to think I'm not bad at avoiding the main thoroughfares. The underground road down what looks like a dead end by the Savoy is particularly thrilling.

That said, much of what I enjoy is in fact driving on the multi-lane roads. I don't dodge around, cutting people up, but I do like knowing the pattern of the traffic flows and choosing my lanes accordingly. The metaphor that often comes to mind is that of a river: it's satisfying, somehow, to know from previous experience where the water always eddies (because of a right-turn lane, for instance) and successfully to pick up the fast-moving current on the left-hand bank. Which makes regulatory interventions that disrupt traffic flow incredibly frustrating. The Lancaster Gate 'roundabout' used to be a trouble-free delight, but now it can take twenty minutes to emerge from Hyde Park. And speaking of the park, why do we need an expensive cycle lane down Park Lane when there's one just inside the railings? One can't help feeling that there are forces at work trying to stop the river running at all. I enjoy cycling very much, but please let's keep the cars flowing, too.

There's another city where the traffic reminds me of flowing water – it's

New York, or more specifically Manhattan. That rectilinear street pattern with its numerous traffic lights creates a very particular set of ebbs and flows. I remember once years ago, late at night, sitting in a yellow cab at a red light on Fifth Avenue. We were high up Central Park, outside the Met, waiting for a wave, and when it came we surfed the greens right down to Broadway. It was a great feeling.

A PASSION FOR SPACE

Ben Okri O.B.E.

(b. 1959. ANTARCTIC TREATY DESIGNATES THE CONTINENT A SCIENTIFIC RESERVE)

Poet, novelist, magical realist, winner of the 1991 Booker Prize.

PUBLIC RITUALS LIKE THE CORONATION have a way of affecting our sense of time and place. They are, in a way, designed to interrupt and reshape our relationship to the social sphere. Since that sphere is going to be altered, whether we like it or not, we must at least make an interruption of our own and plant in this new space some new thoughts about the look and feel of our world.

London at the moment is a city in a constant ferment of building. It is always becoming. Architecturally it is restless. It ought to create structures of habitation, of worship, a place for dreams and work and thought. But more and more its architecture is becoming the enemy of space.

Often the beauty of things is defined by the space around them, and London's empty spaces are part of its greatness. Cities are redeemed by their fields and parks and woods, places where nature balances out the mania to erect, to build, to fill up, the vertical drive to crowd out the horizon. But they have become places where you cannot see far, where you cannot breathe cleanly. They have become functioning tombs. The streets full of cars slowly gas you. The horizon is ringed with tall buildings that increasingly blot out the sky and slowly imprison you.

What we need is an architecture of space, public policy that protects and defends the beauty of empty spaces and rescues London from the fervour of over-building, from the need to turn every available space into real estate. The building of more affordable houses is an important and necessary project. The projects to be wary of are those that take up space while creating value for fewer people.

I love cities for their energy, their variety. They are invaluable for civilisation: where the future is forged, where people of all nations, all colours, all creeds, all orientations come together and mingle and dream. It is where we alter each other and drag the human spirit away from its narrow racial and tribal inclinations into a world spirit that harnesses the collective best in all of us, bringing about something richer for the human race. We need cities to save us from perishing in our own sameness. This is true all over the world.

For a great city to be rich in buildings but poor in spaces is the beginning of that imprisonment of the human spirit which leads in the end to revolt and rebellion. To feel the security of society, decent jobs and wages, to raise our families, to belong to a community, to have legitimate aspirations, are all fundamental urges. But to have all that and to feel oneself in a narrowing world, an increasingly spaceless world, is to feel the tightening of one's humanity. Let's have the vision to protect the magical empty spaces in our city.

GOING PUBLIC

Austin Williams

(b. 1959. LAUNCH OF THE MINI)

Director of The Future Cities Project.

IN MAY 1968, a tower block collapsed in Newham, east London, marking the moment when the UK's housebuilding programme began its terminal decline from a peak of 450,000 homes a year to just 182,000 in 2022. Shoddy workmanship was identified as the practical cause of the structural failure of Ronan Point, but architectural arrogance was seen as the spark. It took a while for architects to rebuild their reputation, but no sooner had they got somewhere than we were told that buildings were responsible for 42% of carbon emissions. They were not only killing people but destroying the planet.

How depressing for a creative profession to be seen, and to see itself, as destructive. Architects recanted their history and promised to be less hubristic. They denounced architecture as potentially harmful; then they purged thoughts of artistic autonomy and critical discretion. A self-flagellating generation of architects has now grown up to counsel the next generation, post-Grenfell, that its impact on the world is potentially catastrophic. It has been a slow journey almost entirely in the wrong direction.

Architects now explicitly accept that their actions can destroy biodiversity, pollute ecosystems and encourage unsustainable lifestyles; that architecture can be safely delivered only through technical means, through regulatory and policy reform that is removed from the grubby uncertainty of public accountability. Those who dissent are often thought to be part of the problem. As a result, many architects have lost contact with the very people – the public – that they fantasise about representing. Name-checking the public is merely a means of justifying a lifestyle-restrictive or carbon-neutral end.

These words are ironic in the context of the Coronation given that, as royalty goes out of its way to encourage less deference, architects seem to want to become a new elite who think of themselves as progressive but look down on those who 'don't get it'. And all in the name of social justice. Architects should be stimulating people's imaginations rather than limiting their choices. For towns and cities to be reinvigorated, we must engage the public in an open conversation about alternative visions for the future.

A LA RECHERCHE DU TEMPS PERDU

Roger Lewis

(b. 1960. WESTMINSTER INTRODUCES THE TRAFFIC WARDEN)

Biographer of Peter Sellers, Laurence Olivier and Anthony Burgess among others.

POETS DWELL ON THINGS GONE AND GOING – a copse of aspens in Gerard Manley Hopkins ('Not spared, not one'); Betjeman's Georgian box pews and Victorian squares, and the City's 'Italianate counting houses, Roman banks'; Larkin's meadows, lanes, guild halls and carved choirs ('all that remains / For us will be concrete and tyres'). Yet the way things were and how they looked does survive, in the background of old films.

The British Transport Films Collection is excruciatingly nostalgic. As gourmet meals are served on the Blue Pullman, for example, England outside the window is at its glorious best: the fields and stations, hedges, agricultural shows, wooden five-bar gates, ploughs, horses, cattle and hares. There are no wind turbines, no nasty housing estates. I can be in tears watching the fish train from Aberdeen and the broccoli train from Cornwall. The sidings, signal boxes, goods wagons, refreshment rooms.

Steam came to an end in 1968, and so at last did the nineteenth-century. Contemporary documentaries show rusty, grimy engines wheezing and clanking in the depots, like dinosaurs in a cave. It was melancholy even then, the piston rods and dripping condensed water, the furnaces. 'Snow falls in the buffet of Aldersgate Station', wrote Betjeman of a demolition job – and everyone seemed in a rush for development and redevelopment and what was called 'urban regeneration'.

This, too, is on the screen. I'm not thinking only of obvious things, like James Mason's *The London Nobody Knows*, filmed in March 1967. Mason had taken a First in Architecture at Cambridge, so was an expert guide to the ruination of alleys and wharves, the pulling down of the Bedford Music Hall, the end of cobbles, iron railings, gas lamps – the end of Sherlock Holmes' London.

But how everything looked is also in the background of *The Spy Who Came in From the Cold* (1966), when Richard Burton, at one with the mouldy stucco, trudges a rainswept Trafalgar Square, Chepstow Road and Queen's Gate Terrace. Or else there's Stanley Baker's *Robbery* (1967) – car chases around a new concrete London. Peter Sellers' *The Optimists* (1973) shows Battersea and Chelsea Creek before gentrification, the Swiss Centre in Coventry Street.

Yet Sixties London is vanishing in its turn. I cherish Richard Seifert's modernistic shapes. I like James Bond-style hotel interiors, where they can be found. That's always what I want from architecture: for it to fulfil my longing for the past. Because if I look about me today, where is anybody's idea of lines of beauty? It's all sheds, fences, sluices, split-level shopping malls, hospitals like cardboard huts, charity shops, solar panels, UPVc windows and doors, traffic congestion, the clutter of cycle racks and ugly shop signs – general dereliction, deliberate dereliction. And it is getting worse. We no longer have architects, only builders. Progress does not mean improvement.

NAMING RIGHTS...AND WRONGS

Tom Bloxham M.B.E.

(b. 1963. PRESIDENT KENNEDY ASSASSINATED)

Founder of Urban Splash, masterly rehabilitators of awkward buildings from abandoned match factories to Sheffield's Park Hill Estate.

HERE'S A QUICK IDEA THAT WOULD COST NOUGHT. Every new building should bear the names of its architect and client in big letters above the entrance. This would make architects and clients think harder about the impact their building will have on the world.

Head offices, shops, even factories developed by the occupier for their own use are often good buildings: strong clients want to say something about themselves, and present their ideas and values, in the buildings they design and occupy. Think Victorian Midland Railway Hotels, David Mellor's cutlery factory in the Peak District, the Vitra Factory near Basel or the BMW Factory in Leipzig. Conversely, speculative buildings, built by faceless clients via committees that try to please everybody, end up as lowest common denominator creations that please no-one. Think endless offices in business parks or volume housebuilder estates designed around cul-de-sacs. Let's make clients and designers announce with pride (or shame) the authorship of our cityscape.

THE LONDON FOREST

Cindy Walters

(b. 1963. THE BEATLES' FIRST LP, 'PLEASE PLEASE ME', RELEASED)

Inaugural winner of The Architects' Journal Woman Architect of the Year Award in 2012, when seventy per cent of her staff were female.

IMAGINE OUR CITIES A HUNDRED YEARS FROM NOW. The big trees planted in the reign of Queen Victoria will be dead. Worse still, we are no longer replacing them; urban land is expensive and big trees need space and costly maintenance. Their absence will change London forever.

Two aspects of this are of particular concern. One is that new developments with little space for big trees are specifying trees with narrow crowns and short life expectancy. At a time when the London plane is at risk from the effects of climate change, this has become a pressing issue. The other is that landscape architects are often brought in late in the day, shoehorning greenery in around the edges of spaces defined by others.

This year, the Architecture Foundation is organising a programme called the London Arboretum that addresses the spatial and cultural role of trees in the city, looking beyond their capacity to mitigate damage to our urban environment to consider how they can give shape and identity to London. One strand will focus on identifying long-established trees, many of them with rich cultural histories: a mulberry planted in Deptford by Peter the Great, a yew in a churchyard in Barnet that was living at the time of Christ. Another output will be a catalogue of trees with urban significance: those at the centre of the 1890s Boundary estate in Shoreditch, planted on a mound composed of the spoil from the slum that previously occupied the site; or the more recent grove of birches that stands in front of Tate Modern, echoing the landscapes of many post-industrial sites.

We enjoy what the Victorians planted for us. In turn, we need to do more for future generations. Let's celebrate the Coronation by planting majestic and resilient trees with broad crowns that will shape London beyond the reign of His Majesty the King.

MENDING BROKEN ARCHITECTURE

Rory Sutherland

(b. 1965. PIZZA EXPRESS OPENS IN LONDON)

*Adman, nudge economist and The Spectator's
laterally-thinking 'Wiki Man'*

NOT ALL THE KING'S PRONOUNCEMENTS have gone down well with the architectural profession. But His Majesty is right about one thing: architecture in these islands is broken. Take residential property, which suffers from what decision scientists call 'choice architecture'. Put simply, the way people seek and choose homes is terrible: terrible for aesthetics, terrible for architects, who presumably wish to create buildings of beauty, and terrible for those who want more sustainable housing. The result is ugly, poorly-built, inefficient homes and profits that largely accrue to landowners, not architects.

How come? Well, most people search for property by choosing a location and adding the number of bedrooms before setting a price. Only then do they look at photographs of the property. Aesthetics, design quality, functionality and even floor area are relegated to the fourth level of choice. Beauty may be in the eye of the beholder, but that requires beauty to be beheld. Under this pattern of selection, the buyer is left choosing between levels of mediocrity.

People also buy houses in a commodified way, largely discounting the effort applied to design and aesthetics. Take the habit of describing homes by the number of bedrooms. Over time this will encourage housebuilders to cram in small bedrooms at the expense of other rooms, such as bathrooms and kitchens. Imagine if people bought art this way. 'I'd like something in oils, mostly green with a hint of blue, featuring three horses and a goat and measuring 9ft by 12ft – for around £200,000.' They would be brought a selection of ten paintings which satisfied these stipulations, of which at least nine and probably all ten would be atrocious. They would select the least awful and end up paying £200,000 for it. Under such a selection path, Picasso would not have become rich. Indeed, no-one would have heard of him.

We can easily change this. And by a method long deployed by kings and princes. Namely a competition, but with hundreds of winners. Britain's leading architects, designers and technologists should compete to produce innovative designs for modern residential housing. The winning designs would be chosen using criteria from energy efficiency and aesthetics to functionality, innovative construction and ingenious use of space. They would be useable by paying a royalty both to the architect, as with Frank Lloyd Wright's Usonian homes, and to the developer, to reward them for building better. Royalties would be payable not by the purchaser but by the landowner through Land Value Capture, a levy on the increase in land value arising from planning permission. Using the designs would significantly increase the odds of planning approval.

The designs could and should be mixed. We can even allow neo-Georgian, mock-Tudor and Modernist. At least one winner should be Indo-Saracenic. There should be microhomes, 3D-printable homes and the odd mansion. But all should be first-rate aesthetically. Consumers would discover that buying an accredited home would give them better quality for no increase in price.

Hence the coronation of a king can be marked not by the construction of one monument but by something more significant: the construction of at least 200,000 magnificent British homes.

TOWARDS SPATIAL JUSTICE

Deborah Saunt

(b. 1965. RACIAL DISCRIMINATION BECOMES ILLEGAL)

Australian-born architect with a special interest in the democratisation of the architectural process. Her designs include a studio for the ceramicist Edmund de Waal.

WHAT IS THE BUILT ENVIRONMENT, if not a cycle of transformation? A process of making, unmaking, and remaking, binding the lives of people, buildings and landscape together in ever new and unexpected ways. We can't halt it, only intervene, and sometimes intervention can mean demolition.

When a building is torn down, its cultural and social aspects are torn down with it. Whether or not the building ought to have been demolished is beside the point; what the process of demolition draws into question is the cultural significance behind any act of construction or deconstruction. For Robert Byron, in 1937, it was 'England and the Empire' that had been 'defrauded of their ancient capital' - by Whitehall leeches, Church spiders, and high finance vampires, to recall a few of those he held responsible.

This is important to consider today. What histories does the built environment give visibility to, who commissioned it, who held power in its creation? Who has a say in how meaning, value and representation are reflected when building places anew? While leeches, spiders and vampires no doubt still exist, we have, between the Coronations of 1937 and 2023 – through civil rights movements, Reclaim the Streets protests and the Equality Act – made great progress in democratising our understanding of public space.

My aspiration is to continue this movement towards spatial justice, towards a built environment in which questions of space, race, health and climate are engaged and advanced in every project. The methodology for realising this is rooted in co-design, the iterative, inductive process of wider engagement that enables everyone to be welcomed – as part of design teams, as clients shaping strategic decisions, as participants in construction and future custodianship.

If we acknowledge that social and material transformation in the built environment is inevitable – that it is part of what draws so many people to cities in the first place – then we must keep our focus on the processes through which this transformation occurs. Only then can we be sure that decisions on the retention, demolition or construction of the built environment are made justly and that the resulting transformation can be celebrated by all.

ROYAL FINE ART COMMISSION REDIVIVUS

The Rt. Hon. Lord Vaizey of Didcot

(b. 1968. STUDENT PROTESTS ROCK PARIS. MORE MODESTLY, A SIT-IN OCCURS
AT HORNSEY ART COLLEGE)

Arts Minister under David Cameron and now a prolific commentator.

IT MAY NOT BE THE MOST ROMANTIC WAY to celebrate a coronation, but the creation of a quango would be one fitting way to mark the crowning of King Charles. The decision in 2010 to effectively abolish the Commission for Architecture and the Built Environment (CABE) was extremely short-sighted. It saved nothing, and set back a decade's worth of work to bring about a more sensitive and thoughtful approach to development and planning.

Our new King has spoken out about many issues that affect our quality of life. His pronouncements on architecture have been strong meat and produced strong reactions. But no one can doubt his interest, or that he is prepared to put his money where his mouth is. Like CABE, he has focused on planning and liveability, and a desire to ensure that new development is built in a way and on a scale that works with people.

It is almost impossible to cut the Gordian knot that ties up planning today - a desire to preserve what we have against an urgent need to build more housing. A planning system - and developers - that put scale and sensitivity at the heart of what they do would at least be progress. And the re-establishment of CABE's predecessor, the Royal Fine Art Commission, would signal an intent to put good design and rigour back into our planning system. There is huge expertise and goodwill waiting to be called upon, and which awaits a platform from which to spread good practice. So yes, let's mark the Coronation with a quango.

VITAL AND VIABLE HIGH STREETS

Ptolemy Dean O.B.E.

(b. 1968. RELEASE OF STANLEY KUBRICK'S '2001: A SPACE ODYSSEY')

Conservation architect and currently
Surveyor of the Fabric of Westminster Abbey.

DURING THE RECENT COVID PANDEMIC, a strange silence descended upon our towns and cities. For many it was a troubling time, but we could at least pause and assess the older towns that had managed to survive the decades-long focus on commercial redevelopment. For once, it was possible to see the ebb and flow of historic buildings along streets that were normally choked by traffic.

The old normality has returned, but things have irretrievably changed. We have glimpsed what urban centres might be like if managed more imaginatively. We can see beyond the pedestrianised areas of large chain stores that are now boarded up, beyond the single-function shopping precincts surrounded by acres of asphalted service yards. We know that the switch to internet shopping has irrevocably cut the demand for deep-plan retail buildings, windowless and reliant on artificial lighting and ventilation. We know too that such places do not readily accommodate alternative uses. And it is equally apparent that the smaller, older or more peripheral centres are the ones alive with people – people, that is, who live locally and who can walk to local services while working from home. Towns and cities where the local high street is directly fed by residential streets are visibly thriving.

Much has been said about the value of streets and value of community. But somehow these messages remain inaudible. Two modes of building still prevail. The first is housing estate suburbia, still following the swirl of cul-de-sac roads. Here, all sense of orientation is lost; and if a clear vista is found, it is only because it is uneconomic to build houses beneath high-voltage power lines. The second, where discomfort of a different sort is found, is the tall housing block. There we find queues gathered at landings at peak times, dreading a lift breakdown.

These towers are unsuitable for those starting families and cannot be much more sustainable in the longer term than acres of suburban sprawl.

Let us revive our high streets and create new ones, linked to residential streets and providing all types of house, in any architectural style, for almost any income range. These developments would remake communities. The new King has been saying all this for years. Perhaps it is time to pay him some attention.

AN END TO DULL RECTANGLES

Thomas Heatherwick C.B.E., R.A.

(b. 1970. AGE OF MAJORITY REDUCED FROM TWENTY-ONE TO EIGHTEEN)

A raw genius whose buildings, town-plans, bridges, buses and sculptures are a catalogue of scintillating creativity.

WHEN ROBERT BYRON REFLECTED on London's architecture in 1937, before George VI's coronation, he criticised the ease with which good old buildings were being demolished and replaced with less interesting ones. Now, as the coronation of Charles III approaches, societies all over the world are living with the legacy of almost a century of these bad, boring buildings.

Too many of the places where we live, work and heal have become miserable and disposable. At their best, these places make us feel nothing. At their worst, they leave us stressed, sick and fearful.

We seem to have forgotten that our emotional response to buildings is a central function of design and also central to their sustainability: if no-one loves a building, it is far more likely to be demolished, rather than adapted.

A century on from Byron's essay, demolition continues to be a huge problem. In the USA alone, one billion square feet of buildings – the equivalent of half of Washington DC – is demolished every year. China generates, annually, over two billion tons of construction and demolition waste. The resulting greenhouse gas emissions are many times higher than those generated by the aviation industry.

It doesn't have to be like this. For millennia, even our humblest buildings went beyond functionality to spark interest, pride and a sense of belonging. In the twentieth century, this changed. Influential figures scorned ornamentation and expressions of cultural diversity. They convinced tastemakers that dullness was clever and that anyone who disagreed was naïve. Buildings that all looked the same began to spring up. And the unsurprising toxic fact emerged that boring buildings were cheaper to build. Dull rectangle after dull rectangle was erected, until billions of us were surrounded by them.

We must solve this problem. Despite all the very real crises that we perpetually use as excuses, the world is wealthier than ever and we are spending more money on buildings than ever. The planet, and we as humans, can no longer afford not to build interesting buildings. As citizens and users, we should demand a world full of architectural diversity that delights and unites us. As makers and designers, we should help create a world where cities reconnect with their essential mission: to provide spaces where people mix, meet, inspire each other and live to their full potential.

BRING BACK DELIGHT

Alison Jackson

(b. 1970. BOEING 747 ENTERS SERVICE)

Photographer, artist and film-maker whose brilliantly fantastical photographs muddle truth and invention while satirising celebrity culture.

I BELIEVE IN A CITYSCAPE which is as visual as it is practical: beautiful, awe-inspiring, exhilarating, a cornucopia of vistas that make you feel inspired and energised. A cityscape of pleasing, exciting and necessary buildings that work aesthetically and function properly, and whose lifespan has been considered beyond thirty years.

Ugly buildings are often only a few design steps away from being beautiful. To achieve delight, designers must consider beauty as a goal, not as by-product. You must arrange, order, find beauty in proportion, symmetry, work to perfection based on architectural principles. Take The Shard, Ground Zero, the Louvre Pyramid, or a Norman Foster building; all different, but each in their own way instructed by aesthetics requiring rational thought and creative genius. Wonderful architecture gives us global cities brimming with culture, heritage, and innovation: arguably Man's greatest achievement.

This is what I see in Manhattan. An intricate skyline and in every block a series of shops that helps life flow: newsagents, tech stores, delis, supermarket, surgeries, bars, restaurants, cafes. All wrapped in architecture that brings delight both individually and collectively. It's the same in Chelsea (the London version), where beautiful terraced houses surround communal gardens and squares, with shops and businesses seamlessly nestling amongst them. Yet driving through much of the rest of London, I see banks of monolithic glass slabs revealing messy interiors and private prisons. Developers, backers and planners seem starved of creativity and aspiration. In consequence, art is removed from architecture.

The look of a city will last longer than our lives. Are we so careless we don't care beyond our time? Or do we want our cities to flourish? As the old Greek proverb has it: 'Humanity is planting trees under whose shade you will never sit.'

FARMSCRAPERS

Carlo Ratti

(b. 1971. DECIMAL CURRENCY INTRODUCED)

Director of MIT's Senseable City Lab, with a special interest in how digital technologies will transform the way we see, inhabit and build cities.

IN 2013, THE NEWLY-CONSTRUCTED 20 FENCHURCH STREET, commonly known as The Walkie-Talkie, inadvertently redirected sunlight into a beam so intense that it melted several cars parked nearby. The news made global headlines but did not alter the rapid pace at which skyscrapers sprouted across London. Today it has thirty-nine skyscrapers taller than 150 meters, with many more in the works.

London, like most of Europe, has been a late adopter of the skyscraper and has not focused much on innovating the form. Its skyscrapers are concentrated in the oldest parts of the city and are ill-suited to the narrow, maze-like streets. The Walkie-Talkie's 'death ray' was extinguished after a sunshade was added to the concave façade that had been acting as a mirror, but the building is still glaringly incongruous in its context. And when these skyscrapers aren't charring windows and burning holes into floor mats, they're rather dull.

How could London push the envelope when building tall? This is not just a rehash of the old debate between architectural universalism and regionalism. Today, the particular and the universal cannot be so easily divided, because every building in every city plays a role in climate change. We need to find a way to make these hulking towers work with nature, from improvements in construction and energy efficiency to more radical solutions. Perhaps – especially with the coronation of a climate-focused monarch – the city could aspire to experiment with its skyline in the quest to develop sustainable infrastructure. If we can revolutionise the skyscraper – the emblematic building of the twentieth century – we can transform it into a building befitting the twenty-first.

Architects and developers are already placing plants along the façades of tall buildings, but these interventions have been largely decorative. They could only improve climate outcomes if built at an unfeasible scale. But we could go further and transform skyscrapers into what might be called farmscrapers. With advances in vertical farming, the facade can be covered with enough square meters of hydroponics to produce hundreds of thousands of kilograms of food annually. This would not replace traditional farming or make cities self-sufficient, but it would provide a new source of fresh food and a much-needed connection to nature. It could even cut the need for air conditioning by reducing incoming sunlight.

There is perhaps no better place than London for the farmscraper idea to take hold. With its myriad community gardens and its breakthroughs in underground farming, it is arguably the world capital of urban agriculture. And London invariably catches the eyes of the world. Instead of dragging them downwards to a comically melted Jaguar, it should beckon them upwards towards a farmscraper capable of inspiring the world for decades to come.

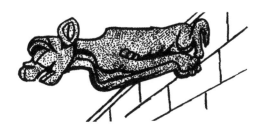

THE WEIGHT OF NET ZERO

Amin Taha

(b. 1974. GOVERNMENT AND UNIONS FIGHT A 'WHO RUNS BRITAIN?' BATTLE)

Architect who saw off Islington Council's threat to demolish his imaginative 15 Clerkenwell Close, leading The Financial Times to call him 'controversial'.

IF YOU HAVE EVER WORKED WITH STRUCTURAL ENGINEERS on road, foot and cycle bridges, you will know the immediate lesson of irreducibility. The span should hold itself together with as little material effort as possible. Apply that lesson to buildings and you'll look at them differently. We might, with Buckminster Fuller, ask: 'How much does your building weigh?'

The facts are surprising. Take reinforced concrete: cement is made from cut limestone, pulverized and burned at 1,600°C for several hours and mixed with various other extractive-based chemicals, in the process losing 60% of limestone's inherent strength and so needing a good amount of steel to help it stand back up: plus excavated aggregate, sharp sand, lots of water and this or that 'admixture' as it churns all the way from cement plant along the highway into town before being poured onto formwork which ends up as landfill. All that processing to achieve the original strength of the same limestone block before it was pulverized and cooked. On a measure of embodied carbon alone, you could have around two hundred and twenty-five stone columns or beams for every one of steel, and sixteen for every one of reinforced concrete. And making 'lightweight' aluminium is an even dirtier process - by far - than making reinforced concrete.

With a conventional steel or concrete frame clad in bricks or stone tiles, the structure needs waterproofing and thermal and fire protection; galvanized steel clamps then penetrate these layers to fix them back to the frame and are then sealed again before being fixed to veneered stone tiles. Substitute all that with a stone frame that serves as superstructure as well as visual finish and the result will be cleaner and cheaper. Combine it with timber for floors, roof structure, internal walls and doors and the outcome is carbon negative: an environmental solution, not a problem, a building that is part of a sequestration industry rather than an industry contributing 40% of man-made CO2.

Note that there has been no mention here of architectural 'style'. Why would there be? That is just material that can be cut and shaped to any form and which comes in a multitude of colours and textures. Familiarize yourself with them, as all architects once did, and your manipulation of them will reflect their properties and your personal skill. To badly paraphrase Giorgio Vasari, this would be to build in an idiosyncratic 'manner', not a generalized 'style'. The ethical end is to restore the idea of *Homo faber* and to achieve greater collective wellbeing. What better way of making architecture?

ON YOUR BIKE

Will Butler-Adams O.B.E.

(b. 1974. MCDONALD'S OPENS IN LONDON)

Managing Director of Brompton, the world's most admired folding-bike manufacturer. Under his direction, Brompton has developed a cult following.

PROGRESS, HEALTH, AND HAPPINESS: the aspiration of monarchs and politicians since time immemorial. With advances in medicine we have seen our life expectancy increase. Our leisure time has exploded as a whirlwind of modern appliances 'better' our lives. All seems fine, but the nirvana of progress is not everlasting, and now the tide is turning. We are facing a global climate crisis, obesity has risen to chronic levels, life expectancy is beginning to decline and so much of the precious space that allowed us to 'live' and flourish in our cities has been tarmacked over to accommodate the explosion of car ownership.

Today, towns and cities are proving to be detrimental to our health. People are caught up in the robotic monotony of the daily commute: travelling underground, drawn down by escalators into dank, cramped, stressful metal tubes or sitting frustrated in square boxes going nowhere, sucking up the pollutants exhaled in front of them. Children breathe polluted air as they study in our urban schools.

Our cities are wonderful places, often the best of civilisation, rich in culture and architecture, full of hidden parks and canals. The distances we travel to move around them are often small, ideal for activities that are good for our hearts and minds, such as walking and cycling. But we need to design and shape them around the people who live in them, putting health, happiness, and freedom first.

The Covid crisis was a tragedy but also a Rubicon moment when urbanites had a glimpse of what life could be, with clean air, fewer cars and more space. Temporary cycle lanes popped up and millions rediscovered the simple delight of the bicycle. Post-Covid, we have not gone back. In fact, we want more, and momentum is growing. Let us hope that, as King Charles begins his reign, we will see greater humanity return to our cities, bringing with it the simple efficiency of walking and cycling as our main ways of getting about.

Published by The Royal Fine Art Commission Trust in May 2023
to mark the Coronation of His Majesty King Charles III
and distributed with *The Architectural Review* and *The Architects' Journal*.

Designed by Julian Roberts
Illustrated by John Broadley
Printed in England at the Buxton Press

ISBN 978-1-3999-4895-1

A CIP record for this book is available from the British Library.